Get It Up

101 Ways to Raise Your Vibration
Reduce Stress, Depression, & Anxiety,
Increase Joy, Peace, & Happiness
and Attract Abundance Automatically!

Original Edition

Sage Wilcox

Get It Up: 101 Ways to Raise Your Vibration, Reduce Stress, Depression, & Anxiety, Increase Joy, Peace, & Happiness and Attract Abundance Automatically!

Copyright © 2016 Sage Wilcox

First Edition

All rights reserved. No part of this book may be reproduced, stored in a retrieval system or transmitted in any form or by any means, electronic, mechanical, photocopying, recording, or otherwise, without the written permission of the publisher.

ISBN-13: 978-1-945290-07-7

ISBN-10: 1-945290-07-2

Library of Congress Control Number: 2016951766

Printed in the United States of America.

DEDICATION

This is dedicated to all of the people who are being diligent and doing their best to better their lives day by day, in every way. Perseverance pays off. Here's to growing your soul. YOU deserve all that you desire and the Universe is designed to make that happen. This book is for you. Enjoy!

CONTENTS

	Preface	i
1	Energy and Vibrations..	1
2	Everything Comes Down to Vibrations...........................	5
3	Your Vibrational Profile...	7
4	The Simple Law of Attraction...	11
5	The Truth Is In the Silence...	15
6	How to Will the Law of Attraction................................	19
7	Fine Tune Your Forces of Attraction............................	21
8	Getting Out of Life What You Put In...........................	25
9	Why Would You Want to Raise Your Vibration?............	27
10	Where Are You on the Spectrum of Vibrations...............	29
11	Questions to Raise Your Vibration................................	35
12	Positive Thoughts Lead to High Vibrations...................	37
13	Meditation..	43
14	Become More Conscious..	49
15	Improving Your Vibration..	59
16	101 Ways to Raise Your Vibration................................	69
17	Law of Attraction Testimonies......................................	73
	Conclusion..	91
	My Blessings..	95
	About the Author..	97

PREFACE

Have you ever looked at the others around you and thought to yourself - *"Wow, things just seem to work for them? I try so hard and for others, things just seem to fall into place. Some people have all the luck, not me, I just don't have any luck."*

It wouldn't be surprising if you have, most of us have thought about this at some point, but there's good news. **Life is not about luck**. You truly do have control over your situation. Rather than luck, the energy we put out there is what causes our situations to occur as they do. This is the energy that others pick up on, the energy that fuels our ability to own our problems, and to take back or lose our personal power. The energy we put out influences our lives so heavily that it dictates our ability to attract things into life that we feel we deserve and feel worthy of.

Consider the old adage:

"The thought manifests the word. The word manifests the deed. The deed hardens into habit. So be mindful of your thoughts and their ways."

I decided to write this book because I've been using the Law of Attraction for several years now, and things in my life just keep getting better and better. But before I learned how to practice and use this universal law, my life was sad, chaotic, and depressing. I attracted a man into my life who cheated on me regularly. I attracted friends who wanted to party like they were in high-school again, even though it didn't feel quite right to me, I attracted a lack of money which caused a whole lot of problems in my life, I attracted a pile of debt that I struggled to pay, I attracted a low paying job that drained the life right out of me and left me limited time with my beautiful children. I attracted a life where someone else was basically raising my kids. I literally saw them for only a few hours each night. I was tired, lonely, scared, depressed, and I cried myself to sleep more often than not. I knew there had to be more, and in desperation one night I begged the Universe to show and guide me. Once I started learning about the Law of Attraction, I couldn't get enough. I purchased every book, article, movie, magazine, CD, DVD, etc. on the subject that I could, and I practiced what I was learning. My life started turning around in amazing ways and I haven't looked back. I will give you examples later on in the book, but one day, after having learned how to master the Law of Attraction, my daughter and I were driving to one of her orthodontist appointments, and we witnessed a squirrel get run over by a car coming from the other direction. It made us sad as we saw the squirrel try to avoid it. As we continued on, we approached a little girl on her bike and we both happened to see her fall. She was okay but she crying hysterically. Next, we hit a red light, and construction, so now we were running late. Then my daughter accidentally stuck the straw all the way through the bottom of her Styrofoam cup causing her favorite drink to spill everywhere. We knew what was going on. We were in a low vibrational state, therefore, more of the same was coming to us. I looked at my daughter, and said: "We need to get it up!" She knew what I meant, so we started talking about things that make us laugh and bring us joy. We started singing and laughing. This was definitely feeling better. We made it to her appointment on time. The orthodontist surprised her with a date to get her braces off. And we stopped for lunch and someone made a random act of kindness and paid our bill for us!

This stuff works, so come along. I want to share the secret to fulfilling all that your heart desires.

With this book, you will discover just how powerful you are and how to utilize that power. The first part of the book is more of the scientific aspect of the Law of Attraction, and the second part discusses more of the actions you can take to achieve your desires effortlessly. Don't let the scientific part of this law frighten you or cause you to lose interest. Stay with it, because understanding it will change your life for the better. Not only have many successful people mastered this simple truth, but they also contribute their success to this straightforward and uncomplicated law.

How far have you traveled in your mind at the invitation

of the eternal question, "Who am I?"

Who you are at your core - the vibrational level, is the template of what you attract. The entire Law of Attraction movement is predicated on that. If you are an agent of change, you will attract change to everything surrounding you. If you are inherently negative, you will attract negative energies. If you are positive, well, you get the point.

The question that then arises is whether you have any control over who you are or is that set in stone? Understand that who you are is not the function of a single phenomenon but an aggregate of environmental conditions that span temporal and physical planes. Some of who you are was determined before you were born, some of who you are is created by outside circumstances and what is going on around you, some of who you are has to do with how you were raised and, some of who you are has to do with the influence other people's belief systems have had on you, and whether you've accepted these beliefs as your own or not. The final analysis of your profile takes all of these things and binds with your desire and your will to be who you want to be. (The definition of the word "will" from Dictionary.com is: Will, noun: The power of choosing one's own actions: to have a strong or a weak will. The act or process of using or asserting one's choice, purpose or determination, to have the will to succeed.) The important thing is to find the harmony of all these forces as you bring the purpose of your life to fruition.

What you see in a person, at any point in time, is just a snapshot of who they are as they transform in all things phenomenal and noumenal; transforming from where they were to where they are going. How much they transform, and how fast, is in direct proportion to how much of their own will they apply to their lives, and to their level of understanding of who they are at any given moment.

Whether you apply the effort demanded by the execution of your will, or you let the winds of circumstance blow, you may be certain of one inescapable fact: You will change. The question is, do you want to have some input into that change, or are you telling life, "Surprise me"?

If you want some input into the changes you experience,

then you definitely need to experience and practice the powers of the Law of Attraction. They call it a law, but actually it's a state, a State of Attraction, where you are always attracting back to you what you are putting out at any given moment. You are vibrating and each emotion and feeling carries with it a frequency. Good thoughts, emotions, and feelings will attract similar things that vibrate at that same frequency. Bad thoughts, emotions, and feelings will attract similar things that resonate on that same frequency.

Once you learn how this works you will begin to recognize it in your everyday life. Here is a simple example, a few days ago I was watching a very sad movie, which I don't normally do because I have learned that depressing movies lower my vibration. But someone else was watching it, and I got sucked into the story line. By the end of the movie, I was bawling my eyes out, and before I knew it I was crying about my dog dying two years ago, about the loss of a loved one 15 years ago, about a mistake I made when I was young, and about a gigantic student loan I am struggling to pay. And I could not seem to stop crying. The sad movie had me in a low vibration, and because of that, I was attracting more low vibration thoughts into my experience. Thankfully, I have learned how this works, so I knew I had to take immediate action and work on slowly raising my vibration up. You have to know that it is a somewhat slow process because you can't jump from despair to ecstasy. It's an emotional scale that you will work your way up or down. There is a ton of information about the vibrational scale, but basically, love, joy, abundance, and appreciation are at the top, hope, optimism, doubt, and pessimism are somewhere in the middle, and fear, grief, lack and depression are at the bottom. But more on this later.

Whether your question is, "Am I the leading edge of the process of evolution?" Or, "Am I more than this form I see in the mirror?" You don't have to wait to reach the end to find the end - the truth, because with a little practice you will find that what is developing is significantly different from what you see life to be.

Most of us have trouble defining our purpose and therefore have even greater trouble figuring out what path to take to get to where we want to go. Many spend their entire lives trying to find their purpose, forgetting that this life is the purpose.

Our being and our purpose are one. Don't take my word for it, but instead, find out for yourself. Certain truths in life must be the fruit of your own labors and this is one of them. This book can only locate the starting point on the path towards understanding. Where you go, how you traverse, or whether you even decide to take it, is entirely up to you.

The starting point on this journey is to understand the true nature of you, your place in this universe, and how you relate to the universe and everything in it.

From personal experience and the experience of witnessing countless others who have taken this path, I can bear testament to the benefits of taking the trip. It is a journey of discovery along a path that varies for each person, yet shares the same destination.

Chinese philosopher, Lao Tzu, said that the journey of a thousand miles begins with the first step. This book is that first step - it poses the questions, sets up the atmosphere, gives direction, and requires you to reflect on what needs to be illuminated within yourself.

Along the journey, and by the time you reach the end of this book, you will understand the central plank that determines the lot in a person's life. You will begin to see that the enlightened person is the architect of his own edifice and that everything a person truly wants is already at his disposal. All he needs to do is ask, artfully.

Unfortunately, this is where most fail. The art of asking is one that is lost to most because we are so dependent on the prevalent form of communication these days - the use of words and audible sound. The oratory fallacy is that speaking is the most efficient means of communication, yet when we attempt to describe something magnificent in nature to another fellow human being, our words are found wanting. And yet we try harder, and harder to get our point across, and finally, we accept that it's not working so we give up in frustration; all the while not knowing how close we came to understanding and mastering this great power. If only we had known that the power of our asking was in its vehicle of delivery, the antithesis of words and sound - silence.

Silence is the clarion of the state of attraction. Words have nothing to do with it. (Unless you learn how to use words to raise your vibration. But more on that later.)

1
ENERGY AND VIBRATIONS

Before the big bang, there was silence. A deep and profound silence that still exists today, enveloping the dark matter that makes up the main body of the universe. Within this silence, comes the matrix that gives rise to energy and matter.

Shift your perspective a little and consider the smallest manifestation of matter that you can think of. In the interest of coherence, let's start with the molecule, let's say a water molecule. Two parts Hydrogen and one-part Oxygen. These are elements. Take Hydrogen and break that down further, you will find a proton, a neutron, and an electron. You will find the same proton, neutron, and electron in oxygen as well, just a different number of them. The same with gold, silver, iron, and any element of the periodic table. Break any proton and neutron and you will find quarks. Keep breaking it down and finally what you come up with is just the vibration of energy.

That's all matter is. At its most fundamental level, matter is not solid, it's just energy vibrating at a certain frequency. Think about that for a minute. One of the things that most people are certain they are certain of, is actually an illusion. Solid, is not actually solid.

The point is that matter is actually just energy vibrating at a certain frequency. That's all that matter is. And it is that vibrational frequency that gives the appearance of being a solid. Everything you see and touch are just packets of energy that are pulled together by a force to keep its state. The strength or quantum of that force determines if the matter manifests as a solid, liquid or gas.

Matter is not exclusive of energy; it is part of energy that manifests as localized phenomena. The balance of the energy manifests as what we see as force. Matter and force are just two parts of energy. You can think of energy as a coin and matter is one side, while force is the other.

Don't let the terms borrowed from quantum physics distract the power of this knowledge. In simple terms it means that everything you see, feel, touch, and beyond, is just energy that has manifested as matter, and it has combined to produce different objects. When hydrogen and oxygen combine, you get water. When carbon combines in some ways it forms coal, when it forms in other ways it forms diamonds. But before carbon was carbon, it was energy - the same energy that combined to result in you and me.

This is profound. When you wrap your head around the fact that you are just a packet of energy, just as the chair you're sitting on, you should begin to realize that you are far more than you appear to be. You are not standing on the earth, you are the same as the earth. The earth is not just in the solar system, it is the same as the solar system; and the solar system is not just in the galaxy, it is the same as the galaxy. And all of it is part and parcel of the universe. In short, you and I are part and parcel of the universe, not separate from it.

Space, time, force, matter, and energy are all a part of who we are.

In the final analysis, we are identical to the cosmos in composition, just arranged differently. It's like fingerprints. We all have fingerprints, they're just arranged differently- and that makes us unique. Just like diamonds and coals which are identical in composition but differ due to formation, we are all essentially the same energy, just arranged differently.

What are the implications of this fact? There are many, but only one is directly relevant to the topic of this book. Because we are identical at the energy level, we can influence energy outside our body, and energy outside our body can influence us.

We can attract things as well as repel them through the manipulation of force. We can command things, or be subservient to them. Forces do one of two things, they either attract or repel. Think of a magnet that is in close proximity. It will either repel or attract. That is the nature of force.

Force is the movement of energy and energy moves in waves. When you see a tsunami, what you are witnessing is a wave that originated from a seismic event out at sea, and the energy that is released from that event is carried by the waves.

In the same way, waves can travel through the atmosphere as well as through the dark matter of space. Not all waves are created in the same way and not all are detectable in the same way. For instance, when you can read someone's mind, those thoughts are energy impulses that travel via waves. If you tune in, and most of us do it by accident, you can actually pick up on what someone is thinking.

The key thing to remember here is that the waves are undetectable by the senses that we have developed over the recent part of our evolution. We have only five senses, and none of these are equipped to detect or manipulate waves and energy.

However, we are still able to control these waves with practice. Once in a while, we happen to stumble upon them and we find amazing results. Through the rest of this book, we will take you step by step into understanding how to recognize these waves and how to use them to your benefit.

It is the cornerstone of the ubiquitous Law of Attraction that everyone knows about, but not everyone knows how to achieve.

2
EVERYTHING COMES DOWN TO VIBRATION

Let's delve into a sort of esoteric concept that might be tricky to grasp right now, but will make perfect sense by the end of this book. *Everything in this universe is composed of energy.* That's right, we've known since 1905 with the introduction of Einstein's "Theory of Relativity" (E= MC squared, remember?) that matter is composed of atoms packed together. But it is force, *energy* that brings the particles that compose the atoms together, and holds this group of atoms together that comprise any object or living creature in the world.

Einstein was able to discover this by breaking down matter into smaller components, calling this the "Law of Vibration." According to him, "nothing rests, everything moves." And the lower the vibration, the slower the atoms, and particles are moving. The higher the vibration, the faster the atoms comprising matter are moving.

So, basically, our bodies are composed of energy that is constantly moving. The force of the energy is packing the atoms in our bodies together. This movement is called frequency. Frequency, in other words, is different levels of vibrating energy. In the seventies, it was proven by a Dr. Colin McClare, a Ph.D. at Oxford University, that the levels of frequency are one hundred times more efficient in relaying information within biological systems than physical signals that humans use to assess a person, place or thing. These physical signals include hormones, neurotransmitters, and other growth factors.

It is interesting to note that we subconsciously "pick up" the vibrations of others, relying on the frequency of vibrations more than our own bodies and conscious minds.

Furthermore, when we look at the concept of "E = MC squared" we see that energy is related to matter and the speed of light. We subconsciously evaluate the levels of frequencies – whether they are vibrating faster or slower. However, all frequencies can be perceived as both colors and sounds.

Wrap your mind around this – there are seven colors in a rainbow, seven notes in a musical scale. Frequency is measured in Hz – Hz determines how fast or high and how slow or low vibrations are. The color blue, associated with creativity, is equivalent to the key of D, the vibration of 587 Hz. How do we know this? Because if frequency is vibrating fast enough, it is released as a color of light.

Because everything is composed of energy, and we are composed of moving atoms, how fast these atoms move manifests itself in physical aspects of life, mental, emotional and spiritual features of our lives as well. The way we feel boils down to how high or low the levels of our frequencies are – how high or low the vibrations of energy are.

Most of us have trouble defining our purpose and therefore have even greater trouble figuring out what path to take to get to where we want to go. Many spend their entire lives trying to find their purpose, forgetting that this life is the purpose.

Our being and our purpose are one. Don't take my word for it, but instead, find out for yourself. Certain truths in life must be the fruit of your own labors and this is one of them. This book can only locate the starting point on the path towards understanding. Where you go, how you traverse, or whether you even decide to take it, is entirely up to you.

The starting point on this journey is to understand the true nature of you, your place in this universe, and how you relate to the universe and everything in it.

From personal experience and the experience of witnessing countless others who have taken this path, I can bear testament to the benefits of taking the trip. It is a journey of discovery along a path that varies for each person, yet shares the same destination.

Chinese philosopher, Lao Tzu, said that the journey of a thousand miles begins with the first step. This book is that first step - it poses the questions, sets up the atmosphere, gives direction, and requires you to reflect on what needs to be illuminated within yourself.

Along the journey, and by the time you reach the end of this book, you will understand the central plank that determines the lot in a person's life. You will begin to see that the enlightened person is the architect of his own edifice and that everything a person truly wants is already at his disposal. All he needs to do is ask, artfully.

Unfortunately, this is where most fail. The art of asking is one that is lost to most because we are so dependent on the prevalent form of communication these days - the use of words and audible sound. The oratory fallacy is that speaking is the most efficient means of communication, yet when we attempt to describe something magnificent in nature to another fellow human being, our words are found wanting. And yet we try harder, and harder to get our point across, and finally, we accept that it's not working so we give up in frustration; all the while not knowing how close we came to understanding and mastering this great power. If only we had known that the power of our asking was in its vehicle of delivery, the antithesis of words and sound - silence.

Silence is the clarion of the state of attraction. Words have nothing to do with it. (Unless you learn how to use words to raise your vibration. But more on that later.)

3
YOUR VIBRATIONAL PROFILE

Your entire being, from the tissue of your beating heart to the tips of your fingernails carry a certain vibration because they are made of matter, and we all know that matter is the vibrational state of energy. Energy can be recomposed to be force and matter. Force has the ability to move matter, and matter can carry force, which you know to be momentum. Think of ice floating in water. The water can move the ice and both are the same thing just at different states of vibration.

Underneath space and time is a fabric that connects every animate and inanimate object, from people to thoughts, from planets to empty space. Science has finally confirmed its existence; something ancient meditation gurus have known all along. In scientific parlance, it is called fields, and each fundamental particle has its own field. A vibration in that field gives rise to the building blocks of matter. When they run tests in the Large Hadron Collider in Switzerland it is not really to find particles, it is to actually find the fields that give rise to these particles. And they have been immensely successful.

By now it must be apparent to you that you are indeed an object that is in a constant state of vibration. Like a tuning fork. Through this field, that's vibrating to make you-you, you are connected to everything else in this universe that is made of energy and matter. You are as connected to your own body as you are to the rock salt buried deep beneath the Himalayas.

This connection to everything and the vibrational profile that makes you-you, and everything else that it is everywhere, is the fundamental basis of the Law of Attraction. By reading this book, you will get a glimpse into the insight that makes this powerful natural law work.

Your vibration is the basis of everything that you do and who you become as you take your steps from cradle to grave. But it is not fully autonomous. It needs input from you to give it direction. Imagine a car going down an incline. It's going to keep going, regardless of your input. It will get to the bottom of the incline. If you take control of the car you can dictate where it will go. In life, you will attract all sorts of things into your experience without even realizing it. The thing you have to learn to do is control where you take the results of this power.

You vibrate at a given frequency no matter what you do. But you can control that through various means. Exercise is one way to control your vibration. Meditation is another. Walking is also a method of manipulating your vibration profile. Each individual has to find the way that bests controls their own vibration. You can set about your task of finding your optimal vibration by discovering what brings you joy, and by balancing it with meditation.

The reason meditation and mindfulness also works, for everyone, is because you can find, through practice, individual meditation strategies that increase your vibration. The optimal vibration is reached when you feel at peace. Meditation automatically brings about the state of peace by raising energies without the practitioner really even having to try. There is nothing to figure out with meditation, it will automatically raise your vibration.

Remember, it's all about the vibration and once you get into the habit of striking the right frequency of vibration, your ability to invoke the leading edge of the Law of Attraction, will come as a natural progression to your efforts. The challenge for most people is finding and making the time to do so, but it's well worth it.

Find a way to make time to be deliberate with where you are at on the vibrational scale. More on the vibrational scale later, but try to find a time each day to be deliberate with what you are thinking and who you are becoming. Have no regrets. Maximize the power you have been given. You were beautiful created, and only you can know what brings you joy, peace, and comfort. This book will help you find ways to do just that. The key is to always remember that you are always vibrating. Your vibrational frequency is going out and like a ripple effect, it is affecting the entire Universe. Every thought, action, word, and deed, therefore, it is very important that you learn how to own your power in regards to these things. You don't have to let whatever thought that just pops into your head stay there. No, you can let it go and think something better for yourself. You have permission to take control of your destiny.

4
THE SIMPLE LAW OF ATTRACTION

You've seen how you can take control of your vibrational frequency and how that can bring you into a state of peace. When we speak of peace in terms of the Law, and in terms of meditation, we are not discussing the lack of war, we are describing the natural state of things. The feeling you get in the depth of your being when everything is exactly where it should be and your mind is as clear as a bell. Peace is a specific state of vibration.

The natural state of things, your point of peace, is characterized by the state of silence. That state of silence does not indicate the cessation of vibration; it just means that the vibration is beyond what our senses can pick up. But you can feel it.

Many who do not meditate stumble upon this state by accident. On a rainy day when the rain creates a rhythm on the window, or when you are stroking your cat and she purrs, you reach a state of exhilarated calm. There are many opportunities to accidentally enter this state, but willfully entering it via the meditation path (or by taking deliberate actions), puts the power of control in your hands.

When you develop the ability to reach the core of silence within you, you come in touch with your vibration. This is where you can make things happen. This is where you attract a life that you decide you want. If you leave the vibration on its own, what it attracts is random and influenced by things you do not control, like what you watch on television or read in a magazine.

You now know where to find it, and get an idea of what it takes to get there. In the next chapter, I will show you how to turn it on at will and how to attract exactly what you want.

The Law in a Nutshell

From a physical perspective, you are what you eat. If you eat healthy, clean food, you will enjoy the benefits of a vibrant mind and a healthy body.

From a quasi-physical perspective, you are what you read. If you consume content that is righteous, you will have a vibrant mind and a healthy lifestyle, this naturally flows to the fact that you are what you think. If you think positively, you will enjoy the benefits of a vibrant life within the ecosystem that surrounds you because you will automatically attract the same vibrations that you emit.

These examples are ones that exist in and around the physical realm of our lives. It is the cause and effect of things that happen in the world we can touch and feel. When you pick up a glass of water and consume it, that has the physical effect of hydrating your body.

There are other realms of life that we can't detect by using senses that are designed to operate in the physical realm. So when you use your eyes and ears to detect something that is outside this physical realm, you're not going to find it. It would be foolish to think just because you don't see it, it's not there. Think infrared pulses that go from your TV remote to the TV sensor. You don't see it, you don't hear it, you don't smell it, you can't feel or touch it, and you can't taste it. But it is certainly there.

In the same way, the deeper realm of your existence, the part of you that connects to the rest of the universe is undetectable by the senses of the physical realm. But they are there. How do we know this? Scientists in England and the United States have found a quantum 'device' buried deep with the physical brain that is said to be able to transmit at the quantum level. Scientists are beginning to realize that this may be the antenna we use to connect with the rest of the universe.

Defining the Meaning and Scope

The Law of Attraction that we are all used to is simple in its definition:

Whatever you are, you attract; whatever you feel, you attract; whatever you desire, you attract. Whatever you are afraid of you attract. Whatever you hate, you attract. Basically, whatever occupies your soul in fervor and intensity, you attract.

This happens because whatever state we are in; we trigger a corresponding vibration. When that vibration is triggered, it attracts similar vibrations back to itself. When you look at that definition, the obvious theme of it is that things that are the same attracts themselves.

The definition is fairly simple but we will break it down in this chapter into its constituent components over this chapter and the course of the remaining chapters.

The first part of being whatever you are, draws on the concept referred to in the Preface chapter of this book. This is the part of you that you have no control over. It is what you are born with and how you are raised. If you were born inherently positive into an inherently negative home, you are going to have a lot of mixed results.

Because of this part of the law, you must make the conscious effort to stay away from drama and negativity. If you think something is against you, it is. If you think you can do it, you can; if you think you can't do it, you can't. It boils down to your mindset and how you condition yourself.

The second part of the definition deals with how you feel. If you feel blue, you're going to attract a lot of negative emotions. There are many people that hear a song on the radio and suddenly start feeling blue, and lo and behold in mere moments, things that deserve the state of being blue come knocking on their door. Then it just compounds with time. Never give in to this. Break out of this as soon as you can. Listen to some uplifting music or go for a workout to break the spiraling situation.

The rest of the parts of the definition follow in the same vein, if you are in a certain way, that's what you will attract. So the point is to be aware of how you are feeling, what you are thinking, and what you believe in. For instance, a lot of people believe in bad luck, especially the kind of bad luck that follows from an event. Let's say breaking a mirror. The actual mirror doesn't do anything, but the person's belief makes them think they will have bad luck and the law of attraction will make sure it happens.

5
THE TRUTH IS IN THE SILENCE

There is also something inside you that is always giving you the option of being and staying who you are or the option to change your life for the better. It's no accident that you picked up this book. The fact that you are reading something about the Law of Attraction says very clearly that something inside of you has been sparked and you want to follow this path to the point that it can have an impact on your life. Even if you cannot verbalize it in your head, you can feel it internally.

If you are just learning about the Law of Attraction and how it works, that doesn't mean that you have never experienced it. You have. You just didn't realize it. There is no way to escape this universal law. Not everything that happens beneath the cerebral surface eventually comes into focus. And when it does come, it is not limited to appearing as thoughts, it can sometimes come as a direct action or an indirect action that can lead to something else.

Have you ever met someone who has no shortage of drama in their lives? If you notice closely, you'll find that they have a penchant for theatrics and exaggeration. These attitudes reflect what is actually happening in their lives. Do you know of someone that seems to have this prolonged string of 'bad luck'? Well, if you study them closely, they too have an affinity towards playing the victim. They have a martyr syndrome that, if left unchecked, will cause them to commit repeated acts of self-sabotage, just so they can maintain this victim mentality that they are accustomed to. Either way, these low vibration frequencies are habits that attract negative consequences.

All these are examples of the law of attraction at work, but not in the positive way you imagine.

The universe does not see things in negative or positive. It just sees what you attract, what frequency you are vibrating at, then it colludes to make it come your way, automatically. The reason there is no negative or positive is because, as humans, we derive something in those binary terms, so as to simplify classification. But in truth, there is no such thing as good or bad. As Hamlet says, "only thinking makes it so." Of course, we have an internal compass, and moral standards that are ingrained in us, but one person's truth can be different from another person's truth. The key is to learn what your moral standards are, what brings you joy, what your truth is, and proceed to accordingly.

There are two dimensions to Hamlet's line. The first is that you can interpret anything you want in a good way or in a bad. The second dimension of that statement is that thinking is what makes things happen, so if you want something to happen, think it in that way, and it will be so. Thoughts are things. Your thoughts actually have a frequency. Every thought you think becomes, therefore, you have to be thinking deliberately and this just takes practice.

Thinking, in this case, is not silence. True silence includes a still mind. The silence that is meant to describe the lack of talking or the lack of conscious articulation puts us in the best position to communicate with the part of us that initiates the attraction process.

The law of attraction can be synthesized as follows, to include all the elements of its tenets.

Whatever happens to you is the result of your request that you placed with the universe at large, regardless of whether you are conscious of the request or not.

Remember the old saying, be careful what you wish for,

you might just get it? Well, my friend, everyone gets every wish they ever make, as long as it doesn't go against the other laws of nature. When you are responsible for pitting two laws of nature against each other, you find dissonance and sorrow. This can be tough, but we need to learn to surrender to the universal laws of nature. For instance, if you wish deeply that those you love would not die, you are pitting the law of attraction against the law of birth and death. This dissonance will come to cause deep pain and sorrow in you. We, of course, need to respect and work with the laws of nature.

Your conscious mind is the part that you are aware of. If someone were to ask you what you are thinking, you would look into the conscious realm of your mind, and tell them what you see transpiring in that part your mental faculties. On the other hand, your subconscious is not something which we can claim to be aware of. I can't really look for the conscious part of my mind and tell you what it's working on at any given moment. The operating language differ between the two realms. But what you do have are those moments of epiphany, where you get it. Those moments seem to come out of nowhere. They seem to come from the silence of the mind and suddenly become apparent.

That silence is like the black hole. It seems innocuous because of its lack of activity, but in reality, it is stronger than all your conscious faculties put together, and then some. Just like the black hole in the center of the galaxy, it has more density than the rest of the galaxy put together.

We need to draw a distinction between a wish and the law of attraction. Wishes, in their most direct sense, have no value whatsoever if the wish is superficial. There is an old wives' tale that you should never reveal your wish, for its verbal articulation causes it to vanish. For all its simplicity and mumbo-jumbo sounding reasoning, there is some truth to it because wishes that come true, come from the silence of the soul.

To make something come true, you sit it in the privacy of your heart, in the silence of its existence. Telling the Universe what you want with your words will not do you any good. You have to learn to think and feel and lift your vibrational frequency up to a vibrational frequency that matches the things you desire. Remember like attracts like.

6
HOW TO WILL THE LAW OF ATTRACTION

Hopefully, you are beginning to get an idea of how to will yourself into invoking the ability to attract the things you want in life and the things you want out of life. You will your desires in life by invoking the silence that envelops your state of peace.

By willing yourself into a state of silence, or a meditative state, you begin the process of traveling from the chaos we all live in with our daily lives and enter the state of peace that is required to vibrate at the right frequency.

In reality, this is going to take a lot of trial and error. I could explain this to you but there are no proper points of reference that could correspond to the words I could use for you to get an accurate picture of what you need to do. Instead, I am going to point you in the right direction and you will eventually learn how to do this with practice.

By willing yourself into a state of silence or joy or peace, you control it in the positive sense. Otherwise, it could trigger a series of events that can even go against your best interest. To take control of it is simple to begin. You have to stay away from anything that could result in negative consequences. Because, unless it violates other laws of nature, the law of attraction will bring about what you desire. Sometimes, unfortunately, that could be something unwanted. Unwanted consequences are usually the result of negative thinking. Excessive fear, worry, greed, gluttony, jealousy, envy, gossip, hatred, anger, etc. are all examples of desires that can influence the law of attraction and bring about negative consequences.

Silence is the voice of attraction, and feeling is the intent or desire. The one thing that will not work in the invocation of the Law, is the use of words and language.

The part of you that is connected to all things in this world, as described earlier, is not learned in English, or Russian, or any language for that matter. You can ask many times, you can repeat your desire silently or loudly and it would make no difference. It is the same with praying, it is what you truly and sincerely ask for, that you get.

Whatever state you are vibrating at, this very moment will begin the process of immediately traveling, reaching out, and bringing back to you, more thoughts and things that carry the exact same wavelength or frequency that is required to match where you are at on the emotional scale. Remember love, joy, abundance, and appreciation are at the top of the emotional scale, with hope, optimism, doubt, and pessimism being somewhere in the middle, and fear, grief, lack and depression are at the bottom.

The Law of Attraction will continually bring back what is required to match the right frequency for you, individually. You can't fool the Law of Attraction into bringing high vibrational things into your experience if you are in a low vibrational state such as worry, anger, lack, or depression.

Unfortunately, some people have formed such low vibrational habits with their thoughts and attitudes, that like a train that can't stop, lower vibrational things just keep coming their way, and it's happening so automatically, that they don't even realize that they are in control of it.

Here's the thing, though, with discipline, you can learn to direct your brain to be in higher vibrational states, therefore, higher vibrational experiences and things will automatically start to come into your life!

7
FINE TUNE YOUR FORCES OF ATTRACTION

Someone once told me that she doesn't dance because she is happy; she dances because she wants to get happy. The simplicity of that concept is amazing. It's an offshoot of a similar statement regarding an outward expression of an inner grace.

Both these aphorisms brilliantly show you the way to change your vibrational state. If you are feeling blue, for instance, you're going to attract some unwanted situations into your path. To avoid that you have the option to consciously change your vibration by doing an outward act to change your vibration. In my friend's case, she chose to dance.

The state of attraction is not just about attracting good fortune and material gain. Although it can be. But using something so powerful exclusively to gain things that don't mean much from a cosmic perspective, is a waste. There is so much more that you can do with the law of attraction than just that.

Stepping up to the state of attraction requires the invocation of a state of peace which you can attain from balancing meditation with physical activity. You can advance that pursuit by also doing a number of outward actions that bring about internal changes in the state of your vibration. This along with meditation, mindfulness, and exercise, elevates your game. But there is more. After all, the universe is abundant in its resources and there is no limit to what you can ask for or what you can achieve.

To fine tune your vibrational state you can add one more outward expression to an inward grace and that is the execution of rituals.

Rituals are directly connected to the law of attraction in the sense that when you believe a certain ritual will bring about an event, you instantly resonate at the frequency that attracts exactly what you want.

Rituals are not ancient mumbo jumbo that have lost its footing in contemporary society. Science has developed methods to research and test the effect of rituals and has come up with statistically relevant evidence that rituals have an effect.

Don't think of rituals as something you find in ancient religions. Every religion, even in the modern sense, has some form of ritual. Look past these and instead, look closely at the coincidence of success in the wake of performed rituals.

Take Alexander the Great, for instance. He hardly lost a battle during his conquest of Asia against the significantly larger Persian forces, and the smaller provincial armies as he trekked to the heart of his adversary's empire. Each account of his battle is more amazing than the previous one but illustrates his ability to overcome great odds. It is well documented in history, how he preceded each campaign with rituals.

Genghis Khan did the same. Even Joe DiMaggio had his own ritual before every fame, as did Wade Boggs and every other major league player.

Rituals are like the tuning fork of nature. It helps, in concert with being in a state of attraction, to amplify the frequency required for effective attraction.

However, do not get carried away with rituals. Some people become obsessed with it and that state of being of obsession alters the vibration and diminishes any potential effects of attraction.

A good way to keep yourself in a state of attraction,

where you are constantly buzzing silently at the right vibrational frequency is to have a daily morning routine. This routine should include meditation, exercise and a simple ritual that gets you into the right vibe.

Fine tuning your state of attraction takes practice and discipline. Both of which need to be slowly cultivated and developed. This vibration is best taught to children so that it becomes second nature to them. It is also easier for kids because they have less mental clutter to deal with it. For adults, fine tuning the state of attraction to the point that it is always in the state of high vibration attraction will have a tremendous impact on their efforts in life.

8
GETTING OUT OF LIFE WHAT YOU PUT IN

Some people may have limiting beliefs holding them back. This is because like energy attracts like energy. For these people, the energy they put out is negative, so the energy they attract is negative as well. Energy perpetuates thoughts, thoughts perpetuate energy. It is a cycle: the negative energy infiltrates their thoughts, and their thoughts create more negative energy.

Negative energy causes feelings of worthlessness and loneliness in some. These disturbing thoughts can cause some people to express negative beliefs, put themselves down, and gossip about others. These negative behaviors and words eventually attract the wrong people into our lives, people who may be described as "toxic." Negative relationships reinforce a lack of self-esteem, therefore, exude more negative energy. Being around negative people causes people who feel worthless and lonely to feel anxious and confused, causing more negative thoughts, more negative words, and more negative relationships. Eventually, this cycle can make you want to throw your hands up in the air and ask yourself "what is causing me to keep befriending these people? It's like I have no luck at all. I might as well give up." And the cycle continues.

This is just one example of how energy powers what you

think, your thinking dictates what you say, thus what you say influences things in your life.

It doesn't have to be this way, though! If you can refocus your energy, let go of the need to know how it will work out, and use positive energy to simply trust that it will, you will find more satisfaction in every aspect of your life and regain the so-called control you feel you have lost. What's more, figuring out when you are feeling bad energy and avoiding it is easier than you think; you just need some practice.

9
WHY WOULD YOU WANT TO RAISE YOUR VIBRATION?

Another interesting thing about vibration is the "Principle of Resonance." When a lower level of vibrations meets a higher level of vibrations, the lower levels of vibrations rise up to meet the higher levels. The implications of this scientific principle are impressive.

Higher vibrations result in feelings of abundance, love, gratitude, freedom and compassion. Lower vibrations result in feelings of despair, loneliness, and confusion. When you raise your vibration in one aspect of your life, the lower vibrations (in other areas of your life) will rise up to meet the higher levels of energy you are putting out on a more consistent basis.

Furthermore, if one person is able to raise their vibration overall, others around them will be affected. Upon meeting you they will feel their vibration rise as well. By raising your vibration, you are not only doing yourself a favor, you are doing good for the universe, raising its overall vibration.

If you are a spiritual person, this is a way to feel closer to God, or to whoever you believe is guiding the universe, because by doing good for others, you are fulfilling the benevolent desire that we love one another. This enhances your spirituality, creates a feeling of joy, and reinforces a healthy attitude of gratitude and abundance.

This book covers a variety of topics relating to vibration. First, it should be provoking questions so you can get a feel for where you are at on the spectrum. Next, I will provide you with several proven tips and ideas on how to raise your own vibration. These ideas will work if you allow them to and find a way to fit some of them into your schedule. In addition, we will be discussing ways to reverse the effects of a negative cycle of habits by taking physical, mental, and emotional actions to raise your vibration.

As we cover topics of meditation and give you pointers on posture and different types of meditation you can try, we will also discuss the importance of living in the now. There are a few easy things you can do *right now* to raise your vibration. Get ready for good things to come your way!

10
WHERE ARE YOU ON THE SPECTRUM OF VIBRATIONS?

The following are two groups of questions about how you feel about things and function in life. Mark down a yes from each group of questions if the answer yes applies to you. Tally up the "yes" marks from each list, and determine if your vibration might be on the higher side or the lower side. (Note that vibrations run on a spectrum – vibrations can be high in one aspect of life but lower in another aspect).

Group One

Are you an apathetic person? In other words, is it hard for you to have compassion for others?

Are you emotionally sensitive?

Is it easy to get under your skin?

Do you tend to take things personally?

Do you often feel "stuck" in life?

Do you experience intense depression or despair regularly?

Do you have difficulty seeing other people's points of view?

Are you unhealthy, ill, or unfit?

Do you have difficulty forgiving – yourself or other people?

Do you often feel guilty or seek things to feel guilty about?

Are you unsure of what you want in life?

Do you perpetually make poor choices?

Is it difficult for you to see beauty in life?

Do you feel unfulfilled?

Do your relationships tend to bring you pain?

Is it easy to bait you into an argument?

Do you complain often?

When you look at life, do you tend to focus on the negative?

Is it hard to feel gratitude?

Do other people find you needy or demanding?

Is your lifestyle more on the unhealthy side? That is, do you eat a lot of processed foods, or take in a lot of violent or intense music?

Are you having trouble making progress in life?

Group Two

Are you aware of the what you say, do, think, and feel, and the way that this affects others?

What about the amount of inspiration in your life?

Can you easily access your creativity and conjure up new ideas?

Are you naturally empathetic?

Is it easy for you to see things from other people's perspective and does the comfort of the others around you, matter?

Are you in touch, or do you strive to be in touch with your spirituality, and deep ideas like love, or life?

Do you feel that you are emotionally balanced?

Do you love to laugh, employ a great sense of humor and tend not to take things too seriously?

Is it naturally easy for you to smile and laugh?

Do you invest time into feeling grateful for what you do have in life?

Are your needs met, and prioritized?

Do you value worldly things less, like objects and material items?

Does self-discipline come naturally to you?

Do you spend time nurturing yourself and others? Are you kind to yourself and others?

Is your life focused on what is presently happening more

than what has happened in the past or what may occur in the future?

Is it easy for you to forgive yourself and others?

Do you lead a healthy lifestyle with positive media, healthy foods and beverages and is your body strong and healthy?

Do you feel a great sense of purpose, like you have found your life's calling?

Are you a patient person who doesn't feel the need to compete or argue with others?

Is a peaceful life more important to you than winning or being right?

Are you open-minded and non-judgmental of other people, their beliefs, ideas, and experiences?

Are you confident in your abilities, in yourself?

Do other people easily open themselves up to you?

Score your yes answers and compare list one with list two. Are there more "yeses" on one of the list? If you answered mostly yes to the questions in list one, your vibration may be lower on the spectrum. If you answered mostly affirmatively to the questions in the second list, your vibration most likely is higher on the spectrum.

If your vibration is typically on the lower side, do not despair! Bear in mind that life isn't seen in black and white and people who do not have higher vibrations aren't "bad people." The great thing is, there are proactive steps you can take today – right now – to raise your vibration.

If your vibration is generally on the higher side, that is wonderful and you have a lot to be thankful for. However, do not make the mistake of labeling others with lower vibrations. Again, life is measured on a spectrum, and even if you do have higher vibrations, more often than not, there are still some things you can learn to improve and control that vibration so that you are utilizing this natural law to your advantage.

With practice, you will be able to pick up on vibrations easily and even make decisions accordingly based on these vibrations. The first thing you might want to consider is thinking in a positive way.

You can research the Vibration Scale yourself, but here is an example of a vibrational spectrum in regards to high vibrations and low vibrations. The Law of Attraction responds to where you are at on the vibrational scale. It's that simple. The key is not to never feel negative emotions, the key is to become aware of where you are at on the vibrational scale while knowing that you will attract more of the same to you.

Very high vibrational frequencies: Enlightenment, peace, joy, love, appreciation enthusiasm, expectancy, bliss, happiness

High vibrational frequencies: Acceptance, faith, eagerness, willingness, hopefulness, optimism, going with the flow, contentment

Low vibrational frequencies: Boredom, fear, worry, just getting by, pride, anger, pessimism, irritation, blame, doubt jealousy

Very low vibrational frequencies: Grief, depression, hatred, shame, suffering, despair

Again, we are always vibrating at a certain frequency, and because we are human, it is normal that it will fluctuate up and down. The goal is to be aware of it and know that the Universe is always giving us back what we are sending out. It can't help but do anything else. It's a law of nature so have fun with it.

11
QUESTIONS TO RAISE YOUR VIBRATION

How to ask Questions Productively that Will Help You to Understand How to Raise Your Vibration

Here is an exercise that can teach you how to tackle the parts of your life that are stressing you out simply by asking productively phrased questions. Asking productive questions is a great way to find and come up with solutions. Once you have asked a solution-oriented question, about your situation, then you should jot down a few different answers that come to you. Go back over your answers and circle or highlight the ones that feel most positive.

Take a piece of paper and write down a question in regards to something that is nagging or stressing you out at the moment. Notice if the question you have written may be perpetuating more negative thoughts. This is very important. A lot of times we can unintentionally create lower vibrational thoughts just by the way we are thinking about something. For example:

"How can I not fail the next math test?"

Take the time to rephrase this question so that it doesn't bring you down. The word "fail" is a lower vibrational word. The way you speak to yourself is extremely important. It will influence how you think, the way you speak to others, and the way you treat others and yourself.

It may take a couple of times to write down the question in a way for it to be asked productively. Every time you rephrase the question, check your feelings. Is the question causing you to worry and feel hopeless? Or is it making you feel empowered and hopeful? Keep on narrowing down the question until it feels like it is at a higher vibration. For example:

"What can I do to expand the knowledge I already have about calculus?"

This question has a high vibration. It makes you feel hopeful, and it acknowledges that you are a worthwhile person who already has a basic knowledge of calculus. These questions are not coming from fear, therefore, make your problems seem easier to tackle.

Now write down ten to twenty answers to the question you wrote down on your paper about what is troubling you. Try not to edit your thoughts, or over analyze the answers you come up with. Then, go ahead and circle three to five answers that feel right to you.

The answers that feel right to you have high vibrations, and because you learned to rephrase the question, it now resonates at a higher vibration, therefore, you will automatically receive an adequate response that matches the higher frequency of the question.

Need a starter question to get you moving? Here is a question that will make you feel happier and can raise vibrations for everyone:

"How can I help make the world a better place?"

12
POSITIVE THOUGHTS LEAD TO HIGH VIBRATIONS

How to Speak to Yourself Positively
"People are not disturbed by events but by the view they hold about them."

The Roman philosopher Epictetus phrased this idea perfectly. An event cannot make you feel a certain way. For example, I recently heard someone say, "rejection *makes* me feel hopeless." This statement is simply illogical.

A more logical way to view rejection is this way: Rejection makes different people feel different ways. Some people feel depression, some feel anger, some even feel relief at being rejected. Rejection does not make anyone feel *one* particular way. What you think and believe about rejection (due to your upbringing, experiences, etc.) will dictate how *you* feel about rejection, therefore, how it will affect you, but it's not the rejection itself. What you have learned about rejection along the way, is not necessarily the truth, therefore, you can change your view of it with practice. The goal is to eventually get to a point where outside circumstances do not affect your emotional state or vibrational frequency.

Which of these statements do you feel would make you feel better about being rejected?

> "I hope I don't get rejected because that would be the worst thing that could happen to me right now. I wouldn't be able to cope, and I'd never get over my ex."

Or...

> "It would be great if my new mate and I stay together forever. However, I am a human being and human beings are fallible. One of us might make a mistake and I acknowledge I may get rejected. If that happens, it would feel uncomfortable, but eventually, I would get over it and start looking for a new mate, bearing the mistakes I made in mind next time. I would learn from it and trust that all things work together for my good."

Statement two, although it is clearly not a naturally occurring subconscious thought, would be the thought about rejection that would allow you to feel better about it. You can practice by deliberately stopping these negative thoughts and rephrasing them with better thoughts, which will assist you in keeping your vibration at a higher level. Therefore, you will avoid more lower vibrational states (and experiences), such as depression, fear, hopelessness, negative people, etc. from being automatically attracted into your life.

Negative Thoughts Are Unhelpful, Untrue, and Fly in the Face of Logic

Not only is statement one, above, unhelpful, but it is untrue and illogical. There are far worse things that could happen. If you allow yourself to believe that statement one is the truth, you will have more problems coping, than if you learn how to train yourself to believe a better way as in statement two.

It is inevitable that bad things are going to happen, and it's normal for people to experience healthy negative emotions for a while when things go wrong. However, if you are still stewing or holding onto anger or pain about whatever it is that disturbed you a couple weeks after, or if you are holding onto a past hurt, or if you find yourself complaining and being pessimistic more often than not, then you can be sure that you are caught in a cycle of negative self-talk.

When you use unhelpful, untrue and illogical thoughts to dictate your feelings, and your feelings to guide your words and actions, things may work out, but most of the time they aren't going to go as well as they could.

For example, say you think that you won't be able to cope with rejection and that you will never get over it. In your next relationship you might act extremely needy or demanding if you feel like getting rejected would be the worst thing that could ever happen to you. You might allow yourself to get walked all over or used because of this fear.

The person who admits that they are human and fallible and accepts that, although rejection will feel uncomfortable, they will get over it is much more likely to be successful in their relationships. They will tend to be more honest and laid back, and will be assertive and healthy in their interactions. Because they realize they are valuable as a human being, therefore, he will not allow himself to be used. If you can get to a place (and you can, with practice), where you learn to trust that everything that happens to us, although uncomfortable at times, is a lesson, your life will be amazing.

Speaking to yourself negatively is not only illogical, unhelpful, and untrue, it can also hurt your chances for success.

Just as you wrote down a vibrational question, write down a statement about what is bothering you the most and re-write it until it is helpful, logical and true.

Below is another simple example. I'm using the subject of math only because I want you to understand how important this is to learn how to apply this to all aspects of your life. Even to the little things.

Low Vibrational Thought/Statement:
I am terrible at math and I'm hopeless. There is no way I will pass this course. I will fail this class which will be unbearable because I would have to take a remedial math course.

High Vibrational Thought/Statement:
I am still learning about this type of math. I wish I would've performed better on the tests, but just because I

did poorly on two math tests, doesn't mean I am hopeless. My math knowledge is just a small part of who I am. No math test can determine my value. Failing this class would be a setback because I would have to take remedial math which would be uncomfortable but I've gotten through far worse situations, so it wouldn't be the end of the world.

To gain practice in thinking at a higher vibration, pause your thoughts when you become aware of them, and write them down. Question how logical they are, and ask yourself if these thoughts are bringing you down and depressing you, or uplifting and inspiring you.

If you need to say the words out loud in an energetic and compelling voice, go for it! It's not the actual words that will raise your vibration, but if the words bring a sense of hope and joy to you, and if by saying them, you feel better, than by all means use this tool. It is what you are actually feeling that causes your vibrational frequency to expand out into the universe where it will mirror, attract, and send back to you things that carry the exact same frequency.

If you like to visualize, see your negative thoughts as one visual and your positive thoughts as another visual and compare the two. You might even personify your inner critic which lowers your self-esteem by giving it a name. It is empowering when you realize that this inner critic is not telling you the truth. Correct your inner critic each and every time it tells you something that isn't true.

Here's another simple example. You may think that you are terrible at math because you failed the first math test the very first semester of school. Is that really a *fact* though? Are you really terrible at math or do you just need to study more? Take the time to really analyze the way you speak to yourself. When you live in the present, and take note of the way you speak to yourself, you may be surprised at how many things you tell yourself that are harmful and at a low vibrational frequency.

-Are you are bad at math based on positive or negative feedback that you have received from other people?

-Are you bad at math because you tried to take the first

test and failed?

-Are you terrible at every type of math and all math? Or do are you struggling in just one section, like calculus.

Re-write the thought until it is true, logical and helpful, then repeat this thought to yourself over and over. This is just a simple example, but you can use this method for every negative belief you have. If you practice this enough, you will begin to think more productively. These exercises, used in conjunction with asking higher vibrational questions when a problem arises are a good way to learn firsthand how to raise the vibration of your thoughts.

It is not your job to never think a negative thought. It is, however, your job to change it once it comes.

Changing the nature of your thoughts takes practice, but it can be done. For me, I felt inspired to stop being opinionated and negative so I decided that every single time an opinion or negative thought popped into my head, I would immediately apologize to the Divine Source and ask for forgiveness. Then I would say a blessing for the person I was judging or thinking negative about. The first few days it was almost a constant battle, but eventually, I was automatically asking the Divine Source to bless everyone who crossed my path without having to think about it first. For example, one day I saw 12 teenagers at a sports event and they were all looking at their cellphones. My first thought was: *How dumb they are all being? They are missing out.* So I apologized right then and there: *I am sorry Divine Source for thinking this way. These are your children, they are on their own journey, and you love them. Please forgive me, and please bless them indeed.* Within two seconds, I saw another teen with a mini skirt on and a shirt showing her cleavage. I could almost see her butt cheeks from the bottom of her skirt, and my initial thought was: *Really? Who dresses like that for a school sports event? Where are her parents? This is so inappropriate.* Of course, I caught myself right away, so I apologized, asked for forgiveness, and said a blessing for the teenager. This happened constantly for almost the first few days. I'd even have to apologize for negative self-talk I caught myself saying.

Eventually, though, I found myself automatically and effortlessly asking the Divine Source to bless others. For example about two weeks later, I was driving along and I saw a pregnant woman smoking. I know that before I had practiced positive thinking, I would've gotten mad and thought and said some very negative things, but when I saw her my very first thought was to ask the Divine Source to bless the beautiful young woman and her unborn child. I was so happy and relieved that my negative thought habit was slowly being transformed and it felt wonderful. You can change any negative habit that you choose with patience, practice, and faith.

One of my clients cut two heart shaped pieces of paper out and carried one with her at all times, and taped the other one to the dashboard of her car. Every time she had a thought that didn't serve her soul she would look at the heart-shaped cutout and immediately change her thinking.

Another client wore a loose elastic band around his wrist, and every time he had a negative thought, he would snap the elastic band and think something positive about the situation instead. He said he changed his way of thinking very quickly with this method.

Your inner guide will give you ideas on what method is best for you. Trust it and follow it. It's the way to raise your vibration and bring better things into your experience.

13
MEDITATION

Here are some tips on meditation and living in the now. Both provide a host of benefits and will make you more productive, happier, and will also raise your vibrations. Read on for some ideas:

Importance of Meditation

For thousands of years, people have been using meditation to quiet their minds and find inner harmony. Meditation helps you concentrate, increases your self-awareness, and helps to fight stress by facilitating the ability to relax and cope with life's problems. Meditation can help insomnia, IBS, PMS, anxiety and panic attacks as well as helping it to control migraines. Studies have shown that meditation can help us in our professional and personal lives.

Meditation Helps You Keep Your Thoughts Under Control

Our minds help us to consciously analyze, plan and communicate ideas. These abilities have helped us to achieve our success and have gotten us to where we are in life today. However, despite the fact that the brain helps us reason, relate to others, and be creative, if we don't learn how to switch it off, it eventually can overwhelm us. If we don't control our thoughts, they can pester us with fear of failure, negative thoughts about our appearance, or worry about opinions that others might have about us. Meditation helps us to quiet this chatter, bringing us relief about these anxieties.

Meditation is for everyone, not just yogis, mystics or philosophers, and here are some tips on how to do it:

Create a Meditation Space

It helps to meditate in the same space every day. Even if you don't have a spare room to meditate in, you can set up a corner or peaceful area in a quiet room that can be reserved for this purpose. You can add a special chair or listen to tranquil sounds like classical music. When you keep the same area for meditation, your brain will learn to associate it with peaceful feelings as soon as you get into the area, putting you into the mindset for meditation.

Learn to Meditate in Other Places

If you simply don't have a quiet area in your home to meditate regularly, there are other places suitable for meditation. If there is nice weather outside, go to the local park. The most important thing to bear in mind is that you want to find a quiet spot where you won't be interrupted. Listen to peaceful music, wear clothes that are comfortable and loose, and stay warm.

Meditate on the Fly

Once you get the hang of meditating, you can really meditate anywhere. (As long as you are not driving or operating heavy machinery, of course.) You can meditate on the subway or train, a bus, or anywhere in between.

Meditation Postures

Seated: You can use a chair, bench or stool to do this posture. Sit up with your back straight, while holding your head and spine in alignment. Rest your hands on your knees or the arms of your chair. Keep your thighs parallel to the floor, and try not to lean against the back of the chair if it has a back.

Cross Legged: Sit on the floor while crossing your legs. Sit upright with your back straight and your head and spine aligned while resting your hands on your knees.

Kneeling Posture: Kneel on the floor with your knees together, buttocks on your heels and your toes almost touching. Keep your back straight, again your head and spine in alignment. Rest your palms on your thighs, and if it feels more comfortable, put a cushion on the backs of your heels.

Lying Down Posture: All you have to do for this posture is lie down on a carpeted floor, towel or mat. Keep your legs straight but relaxed, and let your arms rest comfortably by your sides. This is a great posture if you need to relax or de-stress, but be careful not to fall asleep!

Practice Mindfulness

Mindfulness is a great way to begin meditating. Too many of us run on autopilot, "sleepwalking" our actions through the day, unaware of what is happening around us. Mindfulness helps you to pause your thoughts and reclaim each moment of the day.

To develop mindfulness, you should keep yourself completely in the present moment, notice every sensation and every detail about what is going on around you. Take writing a letter – notice everything about it – the smell of the fresh sheet of paper, the feel of the paper against your hand, the weight of the pen and the feeling of it resting between your fingers. To cultivate mindfulness, try this meditation:

1. Pull your mind away from wherever it is, and purposefully concentrate on whatever you are doing at the moment. Whatever you are doing – walking, eating, taking a shower, begin to do it with all of your senses. Smell the air around you, feel the water against your skin in the shower, taste every mouthful of food you are eating. Ask yourself "what am I doing?" "what am I experiencing and feeling?"

2. After doing this for a little while, chances are your

mind will begin to distract you. This is perfectly fine! Notice the thoughts that come up, but don't follow them. With practice, you will be able to let them go and bring yourself gradually back to the present. Keep this good thing going for as long as you can.

Importance of the Now

Most of the time, we are thinking about the past – either fondly or with regret. Or we are longing, or worrying about the future and planning for it. This isn't always a bad thing, having memories is obviously important, and it is good to plan or develop a contingency plan for the worst case scenario.

The problem with living in the past and future is that we live there, and as places and people become regular things, they become repetitive. Research tells us that if we don't claim our thoughts, we are literally only paying one percent of our attention to the here and now.

The real problem arises when our mind roams freely – we subconsciously think that the past is the present. Past experiences, thoughts, and emotions dictate our current behavior. This automation of behavior guided by the past creates our present, our everyday life.

Then there is the future. We are constantly wandering into the future, thinking "what if?" This distracts us, and we lose focus on what is happening now. When we lose focus, doing our tasks now become more of a burden, frustrating us.

As mentioned before, the universe is comprised of energy, and this energy responds to your energy. When your energy is focused on the past, and the "what ifs" you haven't even bothered to show up to the present universe. The universe won't bother to respond to your lack of energy.

Also, when you pay attention to the now, your experience changes. Whether you call it "the zone," "focus," "single-mindedness" it's all the same. We operate at maximum performance when we are concentrating on what we are doing right here, right now. When you are in the flow, things flow for you. You might find that you are in the right place at the right time, and you are in fact the right person.

When you channel more energy into "now" the universe will respond now. If your energy is scattered all over the place, the universe won't have much to return. When you are more present, this gives you presence. It is easier to attract events and people that are more positive.

Seize control of the present. Use meditation to pause your thoughts when your mind is wandering and bring it back to now. Meditation will give you the discipline that is required to do this, and it is easy to start. Simply see a little more, feel a little more, hear a little more, and smell and taste more of where you are at. Do it now, before you even go on to the next paragraph! Take the time. You will be glad you did. Trust me!

14
BECOME MORE CONSCIOUS

Here are sixty things you can do that will make you a more conscious person. You will be more conscious about your thoughts, how your thoughts make you feel, and more conscious of the world. These are things that will raise your vibrations. It is suggested that you don't put these into some sort of "schedule" or "to do list." Rather, if you catch yourself feeling that your vibrations might be low, or if the thought occurs to you that you would like to raise your vibrations, go ahead and try one of these suggestions:

1. Focus on telling the truth – Those with nothing to hide, hide nothing. To be true to yourself, don't be afraid to tell the truth. If you comply with your pledge to tell the truth, you will naturally be more moral, logical and helpful, so that you have nothing to hide.

2. The next decision you make, take conscious control over it: When people pause their thoughts, and consciously take control over their decisions, particular neural pathways are activated in the brain that help to promote self-control, inner peace and calmness. Besides, any time you let someone make a decision for you, or refuse to take responsibility for your decisions, you become slightly conditioned to be less conscious when it comes to making

the next choice.

3. Make a list of everything that makes you happy and make a point to do these things. Actually acting on the list is the hard part, but happiness will increase your vibrations, and your drive as well.

4. Take inventory of your beliefs. Which are empowering? Choose to reinforce these. On the other hand, purge all beliefs that are leaving you unsatisfying. Changing beliefs becomes easier as you raise your vibrations, and you can change an unsatisfying belief to an empowering one, with practice, using the exercises provided above with vibrational questions and evaluative beliefs.

5. Don't try to run away from your emotions, but be aware of them. Everyone is going to feel sad at some point. When you try to escape negative emotions this could lead to problems like substance abuse or procrastination. If, instead of fighting a depression, you accept what you feel, it will pass sooner if you consciously understand why you are feeling this way. Recognize as humans we will have ups and downs. We need the down moments to help us discover what we want (and don't want) more of. The downs are just indicators for us and help us move in another direction. Be thankful for the direction the down moments give you.

6. Expand your horizons. Try adding something new to any area of your life. Invoke a new habit, hobby, or throw a party. The courage it takes to explore something new will boost your cognitive ability to adapt. This courage will raise your vibrations and help you to push through feelings of fear.

7. Gain wisdom from others. Study the writings of others and apply what you have learned to your life. You can gather the wisdom from a variety of places, someone you speak to face to face, a famous philosopher, websites, or attending seminars. The key is applying what you learn.

8. Realize that everything is a blessing. Bless everything that happens, appreciating the good and the bad, and realize that when supposedly "bad" things happen to us, this is just an opportunity.

9. Be aware of your breathing. Proper breathing occurs when you inhale through your nose and exhale through your mouth. You can bolster your efforts to be more aware of your breathing with meditation and conscious breathing exercises.

10. Always act with compassion. And if you can't muster up any compassion for a person or a situation, then please – do not make any judgments. Making judgments only affects your vibration. Being judgmental and opinionated are low vibrations. Get in the habit of accepting and respecting that everyone is on their own journey.

11. Experiment with different religions if you haven't found one that feels right for you. Get an idea of what practices actually make you feel like your vibration is being raised. Even if you borrow ideas from separate religions, incorporate those religious practices into your life.

12. Invest time in yourself – you are the most precious commodity that you own. Take the time to discover your purpose then draft a plan on how to begin achieving that purpose.

13. Expand your creativity: brainstorming, meditation and creative visualization will help you to do this. We have the gift of creativity to help us solve difficult problems. So if you hone in on this craft, you will be able to raise your vibration by thinking outside of the box.

14. Be courteous to other people. Share your love, positivity and good example. When you are courteous you are raising your vibration through compassion.

15. Be a mediator by resolving conflict between two parties that do not agree with each other. If you are the one involved, and you don't agree with someone else's belief, be the bigger person and stand down. Be an example. Winning an agreement isn't important in the grand scheme of things. But winning on a vibrational level is.

16. Challenge one aspect of your belief system for one week. Either dietary (switch to vegetarianism), spiritual (switch from one religion to another), or emotional (challenge yourself to switch from irritability to grateful), etc. It will raise your vibration and expand your mind. Be open to other ways of doing things.

17. Befriend likeminded people. Being around good people adds joy to your life. If you are going through many spiritual, mental, and emotional changes alone this can be daunting, confusing and difficult. Find other people like you, through a meetup.com meeting or through message boards online or Facebook if you are having trouble meeting like-minded individuals in person.

18. Acting on your desires will raise your vibration, because it encourages us to take action to advance consciously. Compare this to apathy – not caring, which lowers your vibration.

19. Speak wisely and compassionately. Choose words wisely and consciously think while you are in a conversation. People who choose their words show great respect for themselves and compassion for others. If you make a conscious attempt to speak positively, positive results will follow. Be impeccable with your word. Don't just throw words out there. Words are powerful. Use them for good.

20. Face your deepest fears. Fear prevents us from growing and taking other measures to raise our vibration. Facing your fears will equip you with more energy and empower you. What are you afraid of? Go out of your comfort zone and start doing those things. You will surprise yourself with how capable you really are!

21. Spend a day setting a positive example for others in any area of life. This spreads a direct positive message to the minds and lives of others.

22. Accept and love yourself for who you are. The journey of life becomes exponentially much easier and much more rich when you accept who you are. Count your blessings, and accept where you are at with your vibrations Know that at the current moment, you are doing the best that you know how to do, and celebrate!

23. Spend more time with yourself. Meditate, begin a personal routine, tell yourself that you love yourself, go for a walk and listen to your thoughts, think of things you are grateful for or engage in another inspirational activity.

24. Think logically and rationally. Make a point to positively interact with your reality. Remember that

rational thought is a flag for a highly functioning brain. Increase your ability to think rationally by boosting your brain power.

25. Understand that everything changes and that anything can be a reality. Everyone and everything is changing at this moment. Change is undeniable, and it is happening to you and everyone else. You can't prevent change, but you can accept it and work with it.

26. Be open to exploring your consciousness. Whether it's through meditation, trying new activities, exploring your spirituality, traveling or joining new social groups, look into finding new ways to gain a deeper understanding of yourself and your mind.

27. Read a good book. This will enhance your brain power, and the more credible information you retain, the more information your consciousness has to create with.

28. Attend a spiritual retreat – this can be a retreat led by your church, a meditation retreat, or another type of outing.

29. Treat yourself with the respect you deserve, and likewise, respect yourself and your actions. Increase the love you show yourself and others, and express this. Make respectful, intelligent decisions that reflects your values and respect your beliefs intensely. Before you will be able to respect others, you must respect yourself.

30. Express gratitude as much as you possibly can. Daily, at least. Ways to give thanks include before a meal, during prayer, complimenting someone else, or letting someone know you are grateful for them.

31. Take full control of your lifestyle – Sketch out a lifestyle most beneficial to your mental and physical well-being. Are there habits you should get rid of? Are there some habits that might benefit you that you would like to incorporate? Act now! Make the necessary positive changes in your lifestyle step by step to take full conscious control.

32. Realize that you are a spiritual being living in a physical body. Love your soul, respect your body.

33. Write five positive affirmations about yourself and place them on your bathroom mirror. The first thing you will remind yourself of in the morning is how wonderful

you are. What a great way to start the day! Try it and see. At first it might seem or feel foolish, but studies have shown that this simple exercise helps people better their lives in every way.

34. It's time for an upgrade – practice personal development and improve every aspect of your life – your health, your finances and your relationships, to start. Your soul knows what you need to do to improve your life. You are strong and powerful. You can do it!

35. Understand your own thought process and understand it as best as you can. Use meditation to be consciously aware of your thoughts and why you think the way you do. It is possible to create an accurate understanding of reality.

36. Listen more than you speak. You have two ears and one mouth for a reason. Don't interrupt, and don't start talking until you are sure the person you are with has finished speaking. Don't be motivated by your ego and make a pledge to be more aware of others.

37. Start a personal journal. This will help you to be more conscious of your thoughts, feelings, philosophies, what you believe and the actions you take. Understand your current state and watch the progress of this journey. Journaling is a powerful tool for positive transformation.

38. Bear in mind that you are never, ever alone. Somewhere, someone is going through the same thing. Take solace in that.

39. Clear any emotional block that might be hindering you. Work through your powerful emotions about the past through journaling, meditation, talking with a friend, etc.

40. Develop strong people skills. This way you can be more equipped in social situations. Feeling fear in a social context will prevent you from being the real you.

41. Let yourself be inspired, by books, movies, quotes, or others, and then take action based off of the positive inspiration you have experienced. You are inspired by these things for a reason. Move into that inspiration by taking action.

42. Say a prayer and feel connected. The act of closing your eyes and saying a prayer can raise your vibration.

There are many prayers you can say in many different ways; saying a prayer while doing something enhances the power of the message you are sending your consciousness.

43. Pursue a path of spirituality. You don't have to join a specific religion, but being connected to your soul will raise your vibration. Never be afraid to add a new spiritual practice to your tool belt.

44. Avoid physical or verbal fighting or abuse at all costs. Fighting is the opposite of peace, serving only to distract you from raising your vibration.

45. Look at the faults of others "through a mirror." When you see something you don't like in someone else, use them as a learning tool. Take responsibility for what you allow into your focus. What is being displayed? Take that information and make positive changes.

46. Keep your ego in check at all times. Your ego battles your consciousness for power over your mind.

47. Accept people for who they are, and accept their actions. If you try to force changes on someone else, you are causing frustration for both of you.

48. Build up some courage and live in the moment. Do what you want to do, say what you want to say, and live how you want to at every moment.

49. Work on building up your mental focus stamina. This will help you to create a better understanding of reality, and more inner clarity. Mental focus will help you understand others and the world much better.

50. When you set goals, consciously focus on what you are trying to accomplish. Obliterate distractions like fighting, gossip, drugs, and negative relationships. These will always make it harder to raise your vibration.

51. Spend time focused on internal reflection. Put time aside to better understand the thoughts that pass through your head and the emotions you feel in order to provide clarity in your current life situation.

52. Start up a twenty-minute meditation routine every morning, and observe the difference it makes in your understanding of your consciousness.

53. Share your unique insight and wisdom, your perspective, your experience, your purpose and

personality. Writing can be an excellent medium to do this, but you could also express yourself through art, music, and a number of other mediums, even stand-up comedy.

54. Proactively change your belief system and experiment with new beliefs. Find others who you inspire to be like. Find role models and find out what they believe? This will make you more aware of the endless possibilities of life.

55. After experimenting with beliefs, choose beliefs that empower you. When considering a belief, ask yourself how you would feel about adding it to your consciousness. If you feel a connection, go for it. Signs of a connection might be feelings of excitement or happiness.

56. Be positive. Act positive. Think positively. This sets a good example for others and yourself too. Incorporate positivity in to all aspects of your life, because positivity raises your vibration and your higher vibration will cause you to be even more positive.

57. Ask questions about your life each and every day. Work on that knowledge base. Ask internal questions and questions about life in general. Don't just be a spectator of your life. What can you do now?

58. Make other people laugh. Humor helps us to create a positive outlook in life for ourselves and others, and it is rewarding and satisfying. It shifts attention away from painful, negative emotions and moves us towards enjoyment and happiness.

59. Watch your intake of television. What are you watching? What are you putting into your brain? Are you watching programs that are doesn't bring you joy or feel good? This is very important. This is why prominent healers suggest that we do not watch the news (or read the newspaper). Only watch things that have the opportunity of raising your vibration because you will attract similar vibrations to you. If you are watching something, and something in the program starts to feel like a low vibration, shut it off.

60. Push your personal limits. Push yourself to become the best person you can be. Do this in all areas of your life: your relationships, your exercise, your finances,

spirituality, your consciousness. Start pushing in the area where you feel the most soulfully connected. There are many accounts of how all of our thoughts, actions, words, and deeds are recorded and that one day we will be held accountable for all of them. Start being the person you know that you can be – a person you are proud of.

15
IMPROVING YOUR VIBRATION

If all of this feels overwhelming to you, don't worry. With consistent practice, you will pick up on what the best choice is for you and, as with anything you practice, it will become easier and easier. For now, "fake it until you make it." We mentioned that the thought manifests as the word, the word manifests as the deed, and deeds become habits. Faking it until you make it is a whole other subject, but a very powerful tool to use as well. Acting the part literally tricks your brain, and your brain does not know the difference between real or imagined. (This is why you often hear of actors and actresses actually falling in love after they've filmed a movie together. Their brains do not know the difference and they literally fall in love with each other!) Use this simple tool to your advantage in all areas of your life. You will be glad that you did. Note: If you ever feel like you are falling out of love with your partner, all you have to do is act the part, and within just a few weeks, you will be right where you were in the beginning of your relationship.

It makes sense that to get out of a perpetual cycle (where negative thoughts cause negative effects), you need to start by making changes. The changes will improve your speech, and when you speak to yourself enough, letting yourself know that you are a worthy human being who is fallible, your thoughts will change.

Physical manifestations of high and low vibration
Low vibration – When you have a low vibration, you have to face uncomfortable emotions that you believe you have no control over. Anxiety, depression, fear, guilt and other negative emotions affect you and can even cause your breathing to become shallow. The shallow breathing constricts blood flow to your body, making your muscles tight and achy. This, in turn, causes a physical feeling of tiredness and exhaustion. Furthermore, the lack of blood flow limits nourishment to the parts of your body that need it.

Increase Your Physical Vibration
There are a number of things you can physically do to increase your vibration:
Eat nourishing wholesome food
High physical vibrations start with what you put into your body. After all, "you are what you eat." Be sure to get enough protein – this helps your cells grow, maintain, and repair your body (although for most westerners this isn't a problem). Fiber cleanses the body and has many health benefits as well, like lowering blood cholesterol and protecting the body against bowel disorders and diseases. Fiber is found in whole grains, nuts, rice, pulses and cereals.
Some foods can have a tranquilizing effect, keeping you calmer and more positive, increasing your vibration. Calcium, magnesium, and vitamin B6 are some examples. Green leafy vegetables, apricots, nuts, milk/dairy products, and yeast extract are a few examples of food that will make you feel calmer. Meat, eggs, and milk contain tryptophan, an amino acid that becomes serotonin, a brain chemical that regulates sleep and enhances mood.

Avoid Stimulants if You Can
Stimulants like coffee, sugar, tea, and chocolate send the body a burst of energy followed by a quick burnout. They

work by stimulating the adrenal glands that sit on top of your kidneys, releasing a shot of glucose. When you ingest too many stimulants, you get caught in a cycle of needing more of the stimulant to get the same effect and eventually you become dependent on it. Not only do you depend on stimulants to stay alert, but they also contain toxins. The stimulants put your body into a constant state of stress where you fall victim to anxiety, fatigue and mood swings.

The negative feelings perpetuate negative thoughts which lowers your vibration.

You don't have to make a mad dash to overhaul your lifestyle or cut out stimulants of all kinds. Take nutrition one step at a time. If you get good vibrations from a food item in the moment, then eat it. If eating it truly brings you joy, then eat it. Meanwhile, try keeping a food or stimulant journal, and see what triggers good feelings for you along with what doesn't. See if you can make a small replacement at a time. Also, try to make foods associated with higher vibrations more accessible, like putting a bowl of organic fruit out on the kitchen table.

Exercise

Exercise brings a number of benefits to the table for your body, all increasing your vibration.

-Exercise stimulates the appetite and people who exercise tend to eat foods that are more wholesome for the body.

-Exercise makes you feel more confident and capable. As your body gets stronger so does your confidence grow.

-Physical activity releases endorphins, which relaxes you and puts you in a better mood. It also releases adrenaline which stores up in our bodies whenever we are stressed.

-Exercise forces us to make time for ourselves, opening up the opportunity to reflect, meditate and relax.

-Moving your muscles allows the body's systems to work more efficiently which removes toxins.

-Exercise causes deep breathing which is key to relaxation. Deep breathing also supplies more oxygen to the brain.

Although exercise raises your vibration, you don't have to hire a personal trainer or move into the gym. Do what feels right in the moment. If you have ten minutes of free time, take a walk through the neighborhood, take the stairs, or get off of the bus one or two stops earlier on the way to work. I always think of the exercise program called "Walk Away the Pounds." It's simply walking in place in front of your television. It is that simple. Walk in place if that is the only option that you have available at the moment.

Get a Good Night's Sleep
Getting a good night's sleep is essential if you would like to raise your vibration. Not getting enough sleep makes you tired and irritable, which can perpetuate negative thoughts. Sleep is also a process where the body repairs itself during cycles of non-REM sleep. REM sleep is also important because this is when we dream – dreams are our brain's psychological safety valve, which lets us work through problems, anxiety, and emotions so we can start fresh the next day.

-Establishing a night routine will help you get the sleep you deserve.

-Stop work at least one hour before bedtime to soothe your body and relax your muscles.

-It is easier to sleep if you go to bed and wake up at the same time every day.

-Your bedroom should be a safe haven for sleeping. Use your bed only for sleep and sex.

-Bananas, wholemeal crackers, and milk drinks can calm you and induce sleep.

-Although you shouldn't go to bed hungry, try not to eat a large meal before bedtime.

If you are awake at night and can't sleep, live in the moment. Leave your bedroom for another room, read a book or do crossword puzzles until you feel sleepy. Do what feels right for you at the time.

Enjoy Nature
Those of us lucky enough to get to appreciate nature are,

in general, happier and calmer people. In today's era, too many of us live in polluted or overcrowded cities that are noisy. Although concrete may dominate over greenery in your area, you don't have to live in the country to appreciate nature.

-Take a walk through the park on a regular basis. Try to visit the same park each season to appreciate the cycle of nature. Observe the colors of the trees, and the flowers along with the different smells. Breath in deeply, inhaling a large amount of fresh air. Breath in through the nose and exhale out your mouth.

-Spend some time gardening, it is extremely relaxing. The physical tension from your body is released and the act of cultivation is good for the soul. Even if you are a novice, you can enjoy nurturing low-maintenance plants. No room for a garden? Plant a window box!

-Appreciate each season outside. With air conditioning and heating, it is easy to forget to feel the impact of the changing seasons. You will appreciate life much more if you live in harmony with nature's cycle.

1. Spring – a season for starting fresh, clearing your life of clutter, hope, renewal and setting change in motion.

2. Summer – This season brings you a sense of carefreeness and freedom, happiness, and light.

3. Fall – This season is associated with abundance and is time for counting your blessings and reflecting on what you have achieved.

4. Winter – This is a period of time to retreat, enjoy rest, and reflect on and appreciate what has passed.

Show your Gratitude

Appreciating nature gives you a feeling of calmness and abundance. Remember to live in the moment. If you are feeling unhappy by the weather, catch that thought, pause it, and refocus it towards a thought that is more appreciative. Think about how crisp the snow is, how the rain nurtures the earth, or how a thunderstorm clears the air.

Other things you can do to raise your physical vibrations:

-Choose wisely who you spend time with. Being around honest, hardworking, kind, compassionate, peaceful people is a good thing in general. You can pick up on other people's vibrations, so if being around someone is giving you a positive feeling, try to be around them more. With more and more practice, you will be able to figure out and trust the "feelings" of higher vibrations, and what low vibrations feels like, as well.

Raise Your Mental Vibrations
There are practices and activities you can do to raise your mental vibration. Mental vibrations can be associated with your words and sometimes thoughts. Luckily, you have the ability to pause your speech and make it more productive if you feel like what you are saying is negatively impacting your vibrations.

Incorporate Gratitude into Your Vernacular
Gratitude is associated with abundance, which is an emotion that is associated with high vibrations. When you see the bright side of things your levels of stress decrease and your feelings of happiness increase. It is that simple.

How to be More Grateful
First, bring physical cues into your life to remind yourself to be grateful. For example, posting signs and reminders around your house is a great first step. You can write questions or statements such as "What have I received from..." or "I am so grateful for..." You can also put photos up of people, places, and things that you are thankful for. Pledge to stop and feel gratitude for these things every time you pass one of these simple reminders. Your vibration will automatically rise due to this simple exercise, and the Universe will immediately get to work (automatically and effortlessly) to bring you more high vibrational things to match it. It will bring you more things to be grateful for. This is you taking responsibility for your thoughts and vibration. This is you being deliberate. This is you learning to control your vibration. This is you learning how to create exactly what you want in life.

-Keep a gratitude journal, and every day, write down five things to be grateful for. These could be things as small as "I'm grateful it was sunny outside for a little while today. I'm grateful for the warmth of the sun on my face." As you practice more and more every day, finding things to be grateful for will get easier and easier.

-It may be hard at first to feel gratitude when things aren't going so well, but if you go through the motions, it will begin to come more naturally – again, fake it until you make it! Keep your gratitude journal, and if in the moment, you catch yourself thinking negatively, seize control of the disturbing thoughts and turn it around as something to be grateful for:

    -fear can be seen as an opportunity
    -unfairness can be seen as character building
    -sadness can be seen as an opportunity to reflect
    -anger can be seen as motivation to improve
    -negative thoughts and feelings are indicators that we need to move in another direction

Also, as mentioned above, meditation will bolster your efforts to be more grateful, because it helps you to live in the moment as you become more aware and more in control of your thoughts.

Slow down: slow down the pace of your life if you have an opportunity to do so. When you slow down, you may find your ability to concentrate will increase and your productivity will improve. When the speed of your life is slower, you are more in control of your thoughts, your emotions, and your feelings.

One way you can slow down is to set an alarm to go off at different times throughout the day – say, at the beginning and end of work, break time, meal time, etc. When the alarm goes off, take a moment to catch your breath, stretch, and become aware of the present moment using all of your senses as previously discussed.

Take in Positive Media

-If you catch yourself feeling negative, shift your focus towards things that will stimulate your body and mind and increase your vibration: art, music or literature are great outlets to distract you from your troubles.

-If you are feeling negative, focus on positive media. This may seem like common sense, but heavy metal or gangster rap may perpetuate a bad mood if you are already in one. What's more, as discussed above, sounds all have frequencies and vibrations, so certain types of music, musicians, and composers (such as Beethoven) produce positive vibrations in the area they are played, which you can pick up on.

Spend more of Your Free Time Doing Positive Things

-If you have a free moment, rather than watching television or aimlessly surfing the internet, be deliberate and spend your time cultivating positive mental vibrations. Things like painting, being in nature, enjoying art, music, and literature, etc. Expand your mind with hobbies: learn about new subjects, read thought provoking books and discover novel ideas. This will increase mental stamina and the stimulation will leave you feeling more energized.

Increase Your Emotional Vibrations

Dichotomies of High and Low Vibrational Emotions
Fear versus confidence and acceptance
Calmness versus worry
Anger versus forgiveness
Pride versus guilt

Emotional vibrations can be associated with thoughts, moods, and feelings. Here are some ways you can increase your emotional vibration.

Practice Forgiveness

Treat yourself to the practice of forgiveness. Forgiveness is an opportunity to release painful memories and emotions for yourself, thereby increasing your vibration. See forgiveness as a positive thing to do for yourself, not as something someone else has to earn. The more forgiveness you practice; the less negative emotions you will have to retain. Let it go and trust that it was for your good so that you could learn from it.

Consciously Feel and Process Your Feelings

With meditation, you can pause and observe your thoughts. You can do the same thing with your feelings. If you are feeling uncomfortable emotions or feelings, accept that they are a part of life and that this is an opportunity to refocus your words, thoughts, and actions onto something that will increase your vibration.

Keep an Open Mind

The more open you are towards new experiences, beliefs, and people, the richer your life will become. Being open minded opens the door for new possibilities. Remain in the moment, and if this possibility gives you good vibrations, go for it! Remember that with practice comes the ability to quickly pick up on vibrations and the wisdom to decipher which ones are positive for you and which ones when pursued or allowed to remain, will perpetuate lower vibrations.

Increase Your Spiritual Vibrations

Your spiritual vibrations may be associated with how connected you are to your roots, the universe, and your personal power. Meditation is one way to access your spirituality, but there are others things you can do as well.

Be Kind

By being kind to other people, you raise your vibration and theirs as well. Across all religions, the golden rule is embraced – treat people the way you would like to be treated. Spiritual leaders have always encouraged us to be kind and continue to do so, like the Dalai Lama who is often quoted as saying "kindness is my religion."

Be Kind to Yourself

Be kind to yourself as well. Treat yourself the way you want others to treat you. Observe how you feel in the moment and if you are being too hard on yourself about a situation or problem, practice kindness and give yourself a break.

Connect to your inner child – the part of you that is innocent and is still amazed by the world. Bear in mind you are never too old to learn something new, and embrace your zest for life. Try to look at things as if you are seeing them for the very first time.

You Can Begin to Raise your Vibration Right Now

Here are some more steps that you can take to raise your vibrations at this moment. You have already completed the first step which is becoming aware of your vibration. The next thing you can do is take emotional responsibility. Realizing that you don't have to feel anxiety or depression if you put in the work, can be very freeing.

To show your gratitude, jot down five things you are grateful for. Being grateful will come naturally to you after a week or so of practice. Now, ask yourself what you are thinking about. Being more aware of what you are thinking will help you to pause that thought, focus on the now, and put a positive spin on whatever you are feeling. There is always something to be thankful for.

-Take a deep breath. Taking deep full breaths cleanses your body and gives your blood cells the nourishment they need. Shallow breathing can be brought on by emotions associated with low vibrations – stress, anxiety, guilt and fear. The stress causes your breathing to become shallow, which constricts blood flow and makes your muscles feel achy and tired. Taking a deep breath can raise your vibrations right now, reversing the effects of low ones.

16
101 WAYS TO RAISE YOUR VIBRATION

Here is a quick list of things that have the potential of raising your vibration. As you practice these, you will figure out which items bring you the most joy and which do not. Do only those things that bring you joy.

1) Eat healthy
2) Stretch
3) Read
4) Write, keep journals
5) Get up early
6) Actively budget
7) De-clutter
8) Workout
9) Fast
10) Drink water
11) Dress Better
12) Create time to create
13) Save money
14) Coupon more
15) Make lists every day
16) Yoga
17) Less coffee more tea
18) Meditate

19) Be thankful
20) Complement people
21) Morning goal reading
22) Be intentional
23) Tell your loved ones you love them
24) Read a daily devotional
25) Worship your faith
26) Earthing/grounding – Touch your feet to the earth
27) Give to others
28) Smile a lot
29) Plan a trip
30) Think about or watch your favorite movie
31) Cultivate Gratitude
32) Love pets
33) Volunteer your time
34) Identify and release grudges
35) Think positive thoughts
36) Quit a bad habit
37) Stop complaining
38) Stop gossip
39) Get out in nature
40) Fun shows/movies
41) Relax jaw/body
42) Breathe
43) Clean the house
44) Use a water filter
45) Clean out your travel bag, wallet or purse
46) Eat more fiber as a habit
47) Release Judgment of others
48) Watch for beauty
49) Cut back or eliminate alcohol
50) Apologize for past transgressions
51) Pay back old debt
52) Do more than what is asked of you
53) Learn and instruct
54) Create a bucket list
55) Do not eat after 7pm
56) Skip dinner for 40 days
57) Try a juice fast
58) Organize a potluck dinner with friends

59) Juicing as a habit
60) Schedule your priorities
61) Create a rainy day fund
62) Organize and purge your contact lists
63) Sell unwanted items
64) Organize your kitchen pantry
65) Eat more rice
66) Eat more fruit and veggies
67) Mitigate Stress
68) Remove toxic things from your life
69) Use all natural cleaners and soaps
70) Reduce EMF
71) Limit social media / trade for social interaction
72) Take one step at a time / break large projects down
73) Prepare for tomorrow
74) Create emergency fund
75) Try the envelope budget, pay off of debt
76) Appreciate more
77) Thank often
78) There is always more where that came from / be generous
79) Make a great dinner at home
80) Create a fun fund
81) Research your challenges
82) Put 10% into retirement
83) Donate things you don't need or use
84) Feel Generous / keep the flow going
85) Review and replace habits that don't work
86) Write up all expenses without judgment
87) Create a vision board
88) Play with your pet
89) Practice better posture
90) Ask for better deals on purchases
91) Visualize in your mind the way you want things to go and be
92) Clean up old paperwork
93) Organize your bills and schedule
94) Replace negative thoughts with positive equivalents
95) Call your family and stay connected
96) Meet an old friend

97) Practice an art
98) Learn to understand your energy
99) Trust yourself
100) Be courageous
101) Dance / Sing / Move your body
Here are three extras that work:
102) Watch movie bloopers or Funniest Home Videos
103) Make a Laugh Out Loud List (Write down things that make you laugh and carry it with you.)
104) Pray!

Once you get the hang of this, more and more high vibrational ideas will come your way. What raises your vibration may not necessarily raise your best friends vibration, so as you find things that bring you joy, keep track of them. Once you figure out what works, you can put it in your "toolbox" so to speak and have it handy for when needed. And you will need it. That's why this is so important. Life is always throwing stuff at us that we are not expecting, therefore, we need to take control of how we react

17
LAW OF ATTRACTION TESTIMONIES

Here are ten testimonies of how the Law of Attraction works. The first three testimonies I had to add because they serve as reminders that the Universe does not understand whether you *want* something or not, its only job is to mirror back and give you what you are asking for – what you are focused on. Sometimes we unintentionally ask for things that we don't really want by focusing on them. This is why you shouldn't boycott or protest anything. When you focus on something, you are asking for it. Do not worry about getting into a car accident (low vibration), instead visualize yourself reaching your destination safe and sound (high vibration). What you think about most and the vibration it resonates at, is what you will bring into your experience. If you are constantly thinking that our country should not be at war, you will unintentionally bring lower vibrational things into your life. Instead, focus on peace for all nations. What would that look like? Visualize peace. What does that feel like? War equals low vibration. Peace equals high vibration. If you want to stay happily married to your spouse by they are driving you crazy lately, focus on what you love about them. Do not give any attention whatsoever to the things they do that drive you mad. What you focus on, you will get more of. If there are 10 things that your partner does and 9 of those 10 things are driving you crazy, then only focus on and think about the 1 thing you are grateful for. Within a short time, more of those high vibrational qualities will start showing up. I know this can be challenging, but give it a try. It works. It's a law of the universe. There is no way around it.

Be Careful What You Wish For

Testimony 1

Hi Sage, when you asked me to submit an example of how I created my reality with the law of attraction, this situation came to mind. It's not something that I am proud of but I know now that I created it with my thinking. I didn't know how, at the time, to stop thinking about this sexy co-worker of mine. Although she knew I was married, her flirting soon turned into something more one day when she told me that she couldn't stop thinking about me. Ironically, after she told me that, it was I who couldn't stop thinking of her. I wish both of us would've know about the Law of Attraction at the time. When I found myself deleting her texts so that my wife wouldn't see them, I knew deep down that it wasn't going in a good direction. But I loved how exciting this woman made me feel. Even if she did have a bad reputation. I found myself having lunch with her at work, and becoming more and more protective of her. When she started sending me nude pics of herself, I thought I was going to go crazy. I wanted to touch her. I wanted to smell her. I wanted to kiss her. Be careful what you wish for, because you just might get it all and then some. The pic of her fully nude through me over the edge. I literally could not stop thinking about her. Funny thing is, now I know that is exactly why I couldn't get out of this mess. I felt like she was leading me down a path that led to the Devil. I knew I didn't want to go down this road. It's not what I wanted but I didn't know how to stop it. If I had known then what I know now, I would've refocused on my wife and children. I would've distracted myself with other things until the unhealthy habit of constantly thinking about her was gone and had passed. This too shall pass, and I know it would have if I had known that I was the one who was really in control. I was creating my own experience with my thoughts and feelings. Long story short, I had an affair with this woman. My wife, who was my high-school sweetheart, found out and was devastated. My wife took me back several times before I left her and my children for good. It was a nightmare really. I was a coward. I hurt the people I loved the most. I did something I said I would never do. What I focused on, I got. And it's not what I wanted. I knew the whole time it wasn't what I wanted, but I allowed myself to think about her day and night and night and day. I allowed her to keep texting me. I allowed her to punch my wife in the face when we went to tell her to stop bothering me because we were going to work on our marriage. And I allowed her to not treat my children right. I remember telling a friend that sex with my girlfriend was someone weird and awkward, but that sex with my wife had always felt right, like we fit perfectly together. My point here is that the entire time, I knew this woman was not the path I wanted to take, but take it I did because I could not stop focusing on her. The Law of the Universe gave me exactly what I was focused on. I wanted my wife and kids, but I didn't focus on them one bit. I also believe in Karma, and I can see that I am getting what I've given. People, if you are reading this and you have something going on in your life that you don't want, then stop focusing on it. Focus and spend time on what you do want. It's so simple.

Testimony 2
It's funny, Sage, that you emailed me today about submitting a testimony on the Law of Attraction. Let me share my day with you. This morning I woke up late. It's my own fault. I stay up late, therefore, I have a hard time getting out of bed. Because I was running late, I was mad. I knew I'd have to hurry as all get out in order to get out the door on time. And I had to pick up a co-worker no less, so I had that pressure weighing on me as well. My roommate was trying to help me as she could feel the tension in the

air. I was swearing and slamming things. My roommate said "All in God's timing. You're not running that late, so take a few deep breaths. You are doing great." To which I replied, "I'm effing 20 minutes late, I am not doing great! Please stop talking!" As I was rushing around, I stubbed my toe, which only made matters worse. My roommate piped in again. "Try to raise your vibration. You are attracting more of what you are putting out. Think about something funny, quick." Although I knew this to be true I felt justified with my anger so I stayed there and continued swearing and slamming things. As I grabbed my sandals in one hand and held my lunch, briefcase, papers, keys, and drink in the other, I headed out the door in a fuss. Before I reached my car I dropped my phone on the driveway. Quickly picking it up and throwing it in my vehicle, I threw my stuff onto the front seat and slammed the door and basically squealed out of the driveway. When I looked at my phone, I realized that the entire screen shattered. I had the protective glass which was untouched, but underneath it, was a shattered mess. And unfortunately, I didn't purchase the phone insurance. My entire morning went the same way. I spilled my coffee on my white blouse (which was humiliating all day), I got stuck in traffic which made me late for an important meeting, my printer died right as I was printing a report that was due, and later that afternoon while I was at the grocery store I knocked over a display holding a bunch of tea boxes. At that point, I knew I had to stop and take a breath and refocus. I asked myself why I was allowing myself to stay in these low vibrational areas all day. I knew what was happening and I knew that I could change it if I really wanted to. Nobody but me makes me think the thoughts that I do. I carry a Laugh-Out-Loud list that you introduced me to, Sage, so I pulled that out and started reading down it. Immediately I found myself feeling better as I was standing in line chuckling to myself. And would you believe that within minutes I noticed positive changes happening around me? A lady who had a lot in her cart allowed me to go in front of her. And then a handsome man held the door for me and we struck up a nice conversation as we headed to the parking lot. He said he is new to the area, handed me his business card and told me he'd love to connect sometime. I know it is my thoughts and actions that lead to what comes my way. I should have done some relaxation techniques in the morning before I left the house. You can be sure that tonight I am going to bed early.

Testimony 3

I've been married three times. My first two husbands cheated on me. I never cheated on either one of them and would never even consider it. I said that I would never cheat, not only because I couldn't morally do it, but because I know how it feels to be cheated on. It's the most devastating thing ever. My amazing husband and I moved back to our home state because a family member was sick and I applied for a job at a huge law firm in town. I was hired as an office assistant, and I know that I created this job. Every time I drove by this place, I imagined myself working there. Within the first week, at my new job, I got a glimpse of someone walking past me very quickly and out the door. We made eye contact and I realized it was someone I had dated when I was just 17. He was the first boy I had ever spent the night with. I was pleasantly surprised and it was good to see him. He worked in the next building over, so I didn't see him often but one day my supervisor told me to email him and ask him when he might be available to meet with some potential lawyers who had applied to the law firm. I quickly found him in the work email address book, and as I sat down and started to compose my message, I had a hard time not making this a personal email. Memories flooded back into my mind and heart. I asked when he could meet with these applicants, and ended my email with "So, how have you been, anyway?" My heart raced as I hit the send button. Within ten minutes I got his response.
"Hi Julia,
I thought that was you the other day. You stopped me in my tracks.
I can meet with the applicants anytime on Thursday or Friday after 1 p.m. in the conference room.

I'm doing okay, how about you? I've wondered how you've been. Are you still afraid of the dark? Do you still sleep with a nightlight?
Waiting for your response,
Dean"

He remembered that I use to be afraid of the dark. He always made me feel safe.

I scheduled the meetings for him and sent him the day and time, knowing that the conference room was just outside my office and that I would see him on Friday.

When that day came, he walked in looking as handsome as ever in his suit and tie. He always had this air of confidence and strength about him and his blue eyes were captivating. He was talking all things legal with my supervisor when she tried to introduce us. Dean took my hand up to his lips, looked me in the eyes, and said "It's okay. We already know each other. Don't we Julia?"

That was the start of something I knew I didn't want. He was married with five kids, and I was very happily married with three young children. We started emailing each other on a regular basis and he'd even send me gifts through inter-office mail. He started complaining about his marriage and I'd send him articles on how to make things better with his wife. Everything I sent, he would turn around and use it to justify why he shouldn't be with his wife. He gave me many, many reasons why he didn't think he should be with her. Then he started asking me what was wrong in my marriage? When did I notice that I was unhappy? I didn't think that I was. Yes, my husband forgot my birthday at times, and yes, there were several lies that I caught him in throughout our marriage, but other than that we were really a great together. Anyway, this is probably getting way too long, but one day Dean asked me to meet him. We met in a parking lot while talking on our phones. It took me the longest time to get out of my vehicle and into his. He kept telling me through the phone to trust him. He wouldn't hurt me. He kissed me that night, and although it felt wrong, I allowed myself to think about him. At the time, I felt as though he was my best friend and that I could tell him anything. And he continued giving me reasons as to why he couldn't stay with his wife. I was starting to dislike her for treating him as she did. We continued our love letters and little meetings for a few months and one night he asked me to meet him at a house that he was house-sitting for the week. He had it all planned out and we ended up having sex that night. It was far from romantic, and we stopped in the middle of it. I couldn't wait to get out of there, but we left each other with hugs and kisses. He told me that he knew now that everything would be okay then he drove away and back to his wife. A few days later I decided that I couldn't take it anymore. I felt as though I was dying on the inside. I never felt good about what we were doing, and I struggled with it constantly. The universe kept sending me signs to stop what I was doing as well. I realize now that I was attracting the situation into my life. I looked for his Mercedes every morning in the parking lot. I checked the calendar to see when he would be in the building. I checked my email constantly and the interoffice mail several times a day, I read his letters and cards over and over, and I'd look out the window at the end of the day hoping that I would get a glimpse of him leaving. The universe was just giving me what I was so intently focused on.

    I tried to make it right as soon as I could. I told him that I was done and that I was going to tell my husband. I took full responsibility for my actions. I had done wrong. Dean, on the other hand, totally threw me under the bus. He blamed me for the whole thing. He told his wife that it was all my fault and that I had been chasing him. He had a work cell-phone, and he requested that I pay his cell phone bill. The accounting department contacted me and although I had my own cell-phone bill to pay, not to mention I was humiliated, I did pay his cell-phone bill and I apologized to my supervisor. I apologized to everyone for my behavior. I apologized to his wife as well, and she called me every name in the book and told me in detail why my face was ugly. I tried to do everything right to fix the mistakes I had made. It was hard and there were a lot of tears but I had done wrong and I didn't deny that fact. I avoided Dean at work and life went on as I focused on my marriage, thankful that my husband didn't give up on me. Months later I received a promotion at work and was really striving professionally. But after a while, I realized that I should focus on my family even more, so I gave my notice and got done. Dean continued to work at the law firm for another year and a half until he was fired for unprofessionalism. I learned from this experience that is for sure, and I continue to better myself every day.

Ask and You Will Receive

Testimony 4

My husband and I wanted an above ground pool for our backyard. We did our research and also stopped by a few of the local pool places and talked to several sales people. We took home several of the brochures and were trying to decide which one we should purchase. We have four small children, so we were definitely on a budget. The average cost of getting the pool would be between $5000 - $7000. We hated to spend that much, but we knew the kids would really enjoy it. We continued searching and looking at other pools that were similar. We spent a lot of time thinking about getting an above ground pool. For about a month or so, it seems like it was all we thought about. One night, while we were getting ready for bed and still discussing which pool to get, a quick thought popped into my head and I decided to pull Craigslist up on my computer. We had not even thought to look on Craigslist beforehand. I started looking up pools and approximately 30 minutes earlier someone had posted "FREE ABOVE GROUND POOL". My husband almost didn't call because it was just after 9 p.m. but he decided to go ahead since they had just posted it. It turned out the people were getting rid of it because they were in the process of selling their house. Their realtor told them to either treat it and get it up and running or get rid of it. We received a free pool, along with all of the decking and railing to go around it (which was huge), wedding cake steps, the pump, and filter, floats, nets, a vacuum, etc. ALL for FREE! The Universe knew what we wanted, and it delivered it better than we could have expected. We've been using the pool for over 5 years now and it's still going strong!

Testimony 5

I was driving a very old Ford Explorer and I was fine with it, but it was not reliable. My sister was getting married out-of-state so my dad let me take his brand new Ford Expedition. Let me tell you, it was a sweet ride. I was not use to the luxury or options that this vehicle had. My boyfriend and I couldn't even believe how lucky we were to be able to take this sweet ride on a 9 hour trip down the east coast. We were in Heaven and it rode like a charm. We were laughing and loving that we were having this experience together. It was fun! After the weekend, we drove back home and after that, it seemed as though every single new Ford Expedition I passed was waving at me. I seemed to notice them everywhere. I'd tell my boyfriend "Wouldn't it be nice if we could own one of those trucks for ourselves." This went on for weeks, until one day out of the blue, an old friend, who we hadn't talked to in a year or so, called us. He just happened to be a car salesman and he wondered if we'd be interested in a newer but used Ford Expedition that they just got in as a trade. It was a steal. It didn't take us long to decide to go give it a test drive, and it was everything that we had wanted. We couldn't even believe it happened the way it happened, but we definitely feel as though someone was watching and knew what it was we had been thinking about and wanting.

Testimony 6

Here's a Law of Attraction story for you, Sage. I volunteer at a kids camp in my area. The only thing is that I hate to sleep anywhere other than in my own bed. I kept requesting if I could just get to the camp early each morning and leave late at night once all of the kids were in bed. I just wanted to be able to go home each night. They kept telling me no, I would have to stay in the bunkhouse with the other camp counselors. But my house was only a few minutes from the camp! The answer was still no. I dreaded the thought of it. Ever since I was little I just preferred sleeping in my own space. I tried the camp thing once as a child and it was awful. So I didn't let it get me down. I just kept thinking about being able to do the camp counseling with the exception of being able to leave each night to go home. It was my heart's desire that's for sure. Two days before camp was to start, I was told that there were not enough bunks for all of the camp counselors this year and they now needed some people to volunteer to go home each night. I couldn't even believe my "luck". They said this was the first year this has ever happened. It ended up working perfectly for me! Yes! I volunteered to go home each night and sleep in my own bed. Thank you, Universe!

Testimony 7

I've had a secret crush on a guy who goes to my church for over a year and a half. For a while, I'd try to come up with questions to ask him just so I could talk to him. Sometimes I'd get frustrated because there would be weeks where we wouldn't talk at all. I know how the Law of Attraction works, though, and I know getting frustrated is a low vibration that will actually keep what I want from coming to me. So eventually, I decided to give it over to God. I would trust God's timing with everything. If I was meant to be with this gorgeous, funny, talented guy, I could be sure that God had the power to make it happen. I completely let it go. A few months later, my church invited me to a conference out of state. I accepted and was thrilled to be a part of it. I drove the 7-hour drive to the conference with three other women who I was to room with. When we arrived at the hotel we found out that our room only slept 3 so I was told that I'd be sharing a room with my pastor and his wife. This was a blessing in itself as spending time with these two is truly an honor. Because I was rooming with them, they asked if I'd like to join them for a late dinner. They told me there would be four of us. To my surprise, the fourth person to join us was the guy I had a crush on for so long. It was a great dinner and felt very comfortable. We all laughed and enjoyed ourselves. I never would've imagined for any of that to have happened. And although I still don't know what God's plan is for me, this experience was such a pleasant surprise. I feel like because I put my desire out there, and let it go without frustration, things started moving in ways better than I could have even expected them to!

Testimony 8

My first wife and I got divorced because we were not compatible whatsoever. She fell in love with someone else, and cried and cried over this other man. We tried to make it work, but just couldn't. It was just unhealthy and dysfunctional, but after several years of it, we decided to get divorced. She stayed in the house we bought (which I wanted to purchase because it across the street from my Dad.) and I moved into an apartment. I tried to do the right thing as we both moved in two separate directions. I eventually remarried a woman who I got along amazingly well with. Our relationship seemed easy and effortless and I was amazed and appreciated how different and healthy this relationship was. I continued to help my ex pay the bills at the house and I took our two children every Friday – Sunday night and on vacations. I'd even go mow her lawn for her, fix the water heater, and help pay the electric bill. I tried to do what was right. After a while, I couldn't continue to keep paying towards the mortgage as I was paying her over $800 a month in child support. My ex-wife knew that she'd eventually have to move out of the house, but when I suggested that my new wife and I were willing to move in, and take over the mortgage to save it from going into foreclosure, (and also so that I could be close to my dad again), my ex said she'd never let our "cute little family" move into it. She would never allow that to happen. She was nasty and doing things I'd never have expected her to do. But my new wife and I continued to be respectful of her feelings and always tried to do what was best for everyone. Eventually my ex stopped paying the mortgage but I didn't know it, and I kept giving her money for it in hopes that we could sell it and avoid the devastating effects of foreclosure which would force us into bankruptcy. I kept telling her that my wife and I could save it but she didn't want to hear it. She didn't want me to be able to live next door to my Dad because she knew it was what I wanted. She sold everything she could out of the house, saved the money I had given her for the mortgage, and stayed until the bank locked the door. She left that house with $22,000 in savings and there was nothing I could do to save it. It would go into foreclosure and be auctioned off. The house sold and every time I visited my dad I would look over at my old house and wonder what if. My wife told me she was sorry it didn't work out but that we had to trust the Universe's plan. We'd look at the house and admired the beautiful big yard, and the amazing sun the property got. Every time we'd visit we'd say "Wouldn't it be nice if we could've gotten the house back." This went on for almost two years.

One day while we were at my dad's house, helping him split wood, we looked over at my old house and the owner was outside showing it to someone. It seemed as if he was trying to sell it. A few days later an old friend called me, out of the blue, and told me that the current owner was indeed trying to sell it. I knew it didn't sound realistic as my wife and I had just purchased a house ourselves, but I ended up calling the owner and had a conversation with him. I did some research and found out that in order to get approved for the house, we'd have to sell our house within 30 days. It didn't seem like a possibility but my wife and I discussed it and decided to go for it.

It all came together effortlessly! We sold our house within two weeks and in less than two years, I purchased my old house back for $50,000 less than I had previously purchased it for! And my dad was thrilled! Talk about the Law of Attraction. I think as long as we always strive to do the right thing, good things will automatically come to us.

Testimony 9

I'm an older woman, and my last boyfriend and I broke up about 6 years ago. I caught my first husband in our bed with another woman whom he got pregnant, so I had no desire to get married again. I'm an independent woman, own my own home, and have always just wanted to date part time. I've never wanted anything too serious. My children say that my heart had hardened a bit because of my past hurt. I wasn't about to let anyone too close. I would date but at a distance. I felt as though most men couldn't be trusted. My last boyfriend and I dated for 8 years and we always got together on Wednesday and Saturday nights. Although I loved him, we just couldn't make it work. After trying for the 3rd time, we decided to go our separate ways. I'm extremely busy, and volunteer a lot of my time at several different places, but the last 6 years being single have been very lonely. I longed for companionship. I had my daughter sign me up on almost every single dating website out there. I know that she was starting to get frustrated, and to be honest, so was I. I wasn't having any luck at all. I live in a small town that seems to be far away from everything so I decided that I would meet potential dates half way. I drove 30 to 45 minutes and met a couple of men for lunch or dinner, and although some of them were very nice, nothing ever really clicked. I was getting more and more frustrated. I was spending hours online trying to find potential dates. I'd stop over my daughter's house a couple of times a day to check email, but eventually, I came to a place where I accepted that it just wasn't working. I stopped looking online and asked my daughter to check it once a week if she wanted to. After this one-month subscription was over, I was not going to sign up for anything else. No more dating sites for me. At the same time, I was going to a weekly Bible group meeting. I was learning a lot and could tell that I was slowly being transformed in positive ways. It came time for lent (a 40 day fast where you give up something that you know will be hard to do). In the past, I've given up swearing, and chocolate, but I felt like I should sacrifice a little bit more than that this time around. I knew that it was meant to be something that I would really have a hard time doing. I'm not an alcoholic by any means, but ever since I can remember I've made myself one drink with dinner. Every night with dinner I have one drink and I look forward to it. I decided I would give up alcohol for 40 days. And it wasn't easy. Not only was it difficult giving up my one drink a night, but I also had to decline drinks at all of the social events I attended, which are many. Most people were supportive when I told them what I was doing, but some had a hard time with it. They didn't want to drink alone I guess. But I stuck to it, all while counting down the days. I saw some positive changes during my fast. I was sleeping better, and for some reason, my nose wasn't running as much. I was going to the high-school track and walking a few times a week, and one day I met a woman named Susan. Susan was about my age, and we struck up a conversation. She was engaged but had been married before. She said she was married to her first husband for 22 years, and although he was a wonderful person, she just felt as though she needed a change. Susan said she didn't have one bad thing to say about her ex-husband, which I thought was extremely rare, but nice. If only we could all feel that way about our exes. On the 38th day of my fast, my daughter called me and told me that I received an email from a gentleman who wanted to get together. I was spectacle about even replying, but my daughter told me that she would do it for me, and she ended up giving him my cell phone number. Later that day he called me and we talked for over 2 hours. To my pleasant surprise, he lived in the same town as me! And only 5 minutes from my house. We met at a local restaurant and completely hit it off. I've never laughed so much or so hard. One of my first questions to him was why was he divorced? Who had cheated on who anyway? He said no one cheated -his wife just wasn't happy so, he granted her a divorce even though it's not what he wanted. It was hard for me to believe. But a few weeks later, I found out that the woman I met at the track that day, Susan, was his ex-wife! I feel as though the Universe orchestrated it to happen. God knew that I wouldn't be trusting of any man, but I had confirmation from his ex-wife weeks before I had even met him. Some would say it's a small world, or that it was just a coincidence, but I don't think so. God softened my heart to this man before I had even met him. He could be trusted. It's been 5 months now and we are pretty inseparable. As a matter of fact, he is moving in with me, something I wouldn't have even considered with my past boyfriend. We are still laughing and I just can't believe how well we get along. We are extremely compatible and I can't imagine my life without him. For the first time in 40 years, I am madly in love, and I'm not afraid to say so! Life is amazing! Of course, now that I know how the Law of Attraction works, I know that my being frustrated about the dating sites was only keeping me from what I wanted. Frustration is a low vibration, therefore, I was getting more frustration. When I decided to let it go, and trust God, He blessed me even more that I could've imagined or wished for. For over a year I tried dating sites, and went on dates with men that lived two hours away from me. When I decided to trust God's plan (not mine, God's), when I truly decided to trust God's plan I no longer felt frustrated, and I got more than I could've ever hoped for!

Testimony 10

Sage, you asked me to submit a Law of Attraction testimony, and I have had so many wanted things come into my life, I don't know where to start. I've attracted the exact washing machine I wanted, right down to the model number. I did a lot of research and knew what I wanted, unfortunately, my local appliance shop didn't carry it (at least that's what I thought because I was looking at their online inventory). When I called them telling them I was in search of a new washing machine, they rattled off the same model number of the one I wanted. It had just arrived and they hadn't had time to enter it into their system. And to add to my surprise, they said they would match the price of a larger corporation who had it on sale. The same thing happened with my conventional oven. I knew what I wanted and one just became available to me. A few weeks ago I realized that I needed printer paper but didn't have time to go to the store. A friend of my husband's drove in the driveway and he had 11 reams of paper that he wasn't going to use so he wanted to give it to us. Two days later my mom stopped by with two more reams that her friend gave her because she was selling her house and didn't need it! I created a $400 purse that I had been wanting. Surprisingly, my sister-in-law was cleaning out her closet and found a brand new purse, the same brand I wanted, and she gave it to me. We created our car, our cat, our dog, our boat, our hot-tub, not to mention most of the materials we needed to build a camp! Each of these came to us in similar ways. Almost miraculously. Things we knew what we wanted and they just came to us. I have so many more examples as well. We know the law of attraction works so for us we try to always maintain our vibration at a high level. It took us a lot of practice at first, but we think we've mastered it, and boy has it been fun!

Testimony 11

I live in the home state of Patrick Dempsey. He is a few years older than me, and he grew up in a town that is only 30 minutes from where I grew up. His hometown consisted of one traffic light and so did mine. I've always been inspired by his story and his strive for success. And, of course, I've always enjoyed his movies and television shows, as have my two teenage daughters. Patrick heads the Dempsey Center which helps those with cancer and each year my family and I have participated in the Dempsey Challenge – a fundraiser. The first few years my family and I participated, we had a great time, although we didn't get even a glimpse of Patrick, which was fine by us as that wasn't the reason we were there. But then we learned about the Law of Attraction. We were preparing for the Dempsey Challenge as usual, but only one of my daughters decided to participate as my oldest teen had other plans that day. She said "I made my donation, but I'm not going to go this year. It's not like we are going to see Patrick anyway." My other daughter and I decided to stay in a high vibration, and we thanked the Universe for allowing us to meet Patrick, although we wouldn't get frustrated if we didn't. We put it out there, and now it was our job to have fun and trust. After we walked the 5K run, which was a blast, we went to the food tent to get a snack. We didn't see Patrick anywhere, but we had fun and were ready to head home. All of the sudden, Patrick walked by. My daughter stood up, looking his way, and Patrick noticed her. As if reading her mind, he asked if she'd like a picture taken with him. He was extremely nice and kind and he asked how we were doing. We weren't expecting this at all, so we didn't have our camera ready and we knew we had to hurry as his people were rushing him along. So my husband whipped out his cellphone and took a quick photo. It came out great and we were on cloud nine. We could not even believe what had just happened! We showed our oldest daughter and although happy for her sister she was so bummed that she had missed it. The following year, my husband had a co-worker who had a team that had raised $10,000 for the Dempsey Challenge, and because of that, the team received tickets to a private luncheon with Patrick. Unfortunately, no one on the team was able to go so they all decided together that my husband should receive the tickets! We were all able to meet Patrick in a more personable setting and have more photos taken with him. It's so crazy what wonderful things can happen when we learn to trust the universe and just do our job of maintaining a high vibration free from complaining, envy, and frustration but full of gratitude, love, and ease.

Testimony 12

I have a testimony you might not believe. I'm a single mom of two. I work full time but it doesn't seem hardly enough as I try to keep my head above water. Let's just say, I haven't had an easy go of it. My ex isn't involved, lives out of state, and rarely sees our children. He was, however, paying child support until he hurt himself and became disabled a few years back. The child support stopped and I didn't know what I was going to do. After that, I was on the verge of losing my house for two years straight but somehow managed to keep at it. Barely. Winters were the hardest as I try to pay for propane, and my electricity was only shut off a few times. My oldest son graduated from high school two years ago and had moved into his own apartment. My oldest daughter was in her junior year of high-school and my only hope and goal was to try to maintain our living arrangements long enough for her to graduate from high-school. Each month I wondered if we would have to move. I thought about having my daughter live with my brother (who lived right down the road) just so that she could stay in the same town and be able to continue to stay in the same school system that she had since kindergarten. I cried myself to sleep many nights wondering what I was going to do. Our house stayed at 57 degrees in the winter, and we tried to keep the electricity to a bare minimum. I could not afford my mortgage but I couldn't imagine making my daughter have to switch schools during her senior year. She was petrified and so was I. How was I going to make it another year like this? I tried to visualize how I wanted it to go. I tried to say positive affirmations. I know about vibrations and that I am creating my reality, and I was doing what I could to remain hopeful but at times it seemed useless. Until one day, I received a notice in the mail from my mortgage company. There had been some huge mix up that the mortgage company was responsible for. Something to do with having lost the deeds to some of the properties, and although this didn't affect many people, it did affect me and my mortgage. The notice said that I wouldn't have to pay my mortgage until the matter was cleared up. I lived for over a year without having to pay the mortgage! What are the odds of that? I couldn't even believe it. My daughter graduated in June, and the matter got cleared up in September. I had to start repaying my mortgage a few days after my daughter moved into her college dorm. My dream was fulfilled and I was able to sell my house and move to another area.

CONCLUSION

Your Journey Starts with One Step
In this Book, we discussed 101 things you can do to raise your vibration. We spoke about breaking down the negativity cycle by changing our thoughts first, then our actions, then our emotions. Nothing will change until you learn how to change your thoughts. We think 90% of the same thoughts we thought yesterday, therefore, we continue to create more of the same. We have to learn how to think differently if we want to see different results. You have to become aware of what you are thinking, and change it to something more beneficial. If a thought isn't doing you good, then stop thinking it. At first, it will feel as if this is impossible, but trust me, it is possible. Many people have mastered it, and so will you.

We also spoke about the importance of living in the now, meditation, and how to speak to yourself positively.

Again, if you practice these things consistently keeping your vibration high will become second nature for you. You will find yourself being more productive, more grateful, and all around more positive as you make these changes. And you will notice when things happen and why. You will also notice higher vibrational things and experiences coming your way.

Your energy will be high and you will get out of the universe what you put into it. We hope you enjoyed this book and encourage you to make some of these changes, or at least consider them food for thought. This book did not come into your experience by accident. You are meant to discover this simple law of the universe. Your inner being wants all that you desire to fully manifest for you.

Just as the voice of a person must be converted to radio waves for it to be broadcast across the airwaves, so to must the call to inspire the power of attraction be converted from conscious desire to vibrational communication. You must will the conversion from words to feelings. These feelings are not the emotions we so often confuse with feeling, but they are akin to the sense of knowing, the sense of communicating with something that is whole, complete and all encompassing.

There are layers to this existence that we are just beginning to cobble together in our consciousness. I suspect we have some way to go, but for now, we seem to have instinctively recognized that there is something more, something that transcends the physical world we observe with our senses.

The wise among us have seen deeper and found a totally different universe where the rules are in contradiction yet manage to live in harmony. It's like the physical universe and the quantum universe, where everything that we thought we knew is out the window.

In this universe, it is silence that commands and holds life. We find strength and unity in this silence and it gives a whole new meaning to those times we heard our parents preach that "silence is golden." We stop the random thoughts that come at us from every direction, become silent, then deliberately focus on a vibration that we want to attract to ourselves.

There needs to be a shift in perspective so that we can bring the truth of how the universe, which includes us and everything around us, really works. We are so caught up with the material aspect of what we see that it's easy to think that everything has a solid form to it. But it doesn't. At the most basic level even that which appears solid is actually energy, and that is exactly what Einstein figured out when he gave us $E=MC_2$ which means matter can be converted to energy and vice versa.

That understanding makes the law of attraction *seem* real. But it really is, it doesn't have to stop at seeming real. The law of attraction has been proven repeatedly, and you have done it too, unwittingly. Reflect, and you will know this to be true.

Space and time, force and matter are all derivations of energy, and it makes up who we are. It is because of this relationship that we are able to attract and repel based on how we vibrate. Psychologically this is an important point to note. If we subconsciously hate something we are going to attract it in a different way. We may actually end up bringing that situation into our lives thereby making an imaginary fear or revulsion, real.

In the execution of the law of attraction, a person's mindset is important, and so is their ability to center themselves in the event of distractions. One of the biggest distractions in the execution of the state of attraction is the fallacy of expectation.

There are a number of new age materials that equivocally champions the use of expectations to force an outcome. When you use the law of attraction stay away from expectations and you will find a better success rate.

Instead of expectations, use faith instead. Faith is not something that hints at blind expectations. Faith requires that you work at something and let it take its course. Faith is not easily explained. Faith is not the same state of being as when you are making a wish. Faith is the understanding that everything is what it is and trusting that things will come as they should. It is the hope and assurance of things unseen.

Faith is the knowledge that the law of nature is fair and balanced and is not out to get you. You are given access to the law of attraction, just as you are subjected to the laws of the universe.

If you develop the proper mindset, resonate at the silent frequency of peace and keep yourself in a high vibrational state of attraction, then faith is the knowledge that whatever you ask for within the laws of nature will set your feet on the path to attain it.

You are the reflection of the universe that you occupy, and you, and everything around you, is connected by the inextricable link. Because you are connected, when you reach out to embrace whatever you need, it will come.

Have fun with this, because fun is a high vibration, and please feel free to contact me with your very own Law of Attraction testimonies.

Get It Up (and keep it up!)

MY BLESSINGS

When I was eleven years old or so, I remember sitting outside my childhood home. It was a cool summer day and the trees were blowing gently. I remember feeling as though the Divine Source was communicating with me. It was subtle, but it was there. I didn't feel alone and I felt cared for. My parents divorced when I was four and I didn't see my father often. Neither one of my parents were religious, and we never went to church. So this sensation that I was feeling didn't come from my upbringing. I felt connected. I feel as though the Divine Source has always been calling me to come closer. Of course, there were several years that, although I prayed, I didn't really follow The Word. I strayed time and time again, and I've always known when I've done so. I thought my first marriage was great, but it was far from it. I cried the last year of our marriage. One night, while my husband was out with another woman, and I lay home awake in our bed, pregnant, I called out to the Divine Source asking for it to please ease the pain that was consuming me. Almost immediately I felt relief wash over me. I knew that I wasn't alone. We had been married for five years and not only were we expecting, but we had a beautiful 3-year-old daughter as well. This pain went on and on as I tried to figure out what I should do. Our second daughter was born and we gave her the middle name: Hope as in hope for our marriage. My husband worked late bartending, therefore, I got up early each morning and got our daughters ready for daycare. I worked 45 minutes from home so I left our apartment each morning at 6:45 a.m. and I arrived home each night at 6 p.m. On my breaks at work, I would pump my breast milk and cry for my babies. After my first daughter was born, I longed to stay home. I even lied about needing an extra unpaid week off due to not healing correctly after my C-section. It wasn't true but I couldn't bear to leave my newborn. It broke my heart. I researched jobs at home, but I found nothing and had to go back to work. Eventually, my husband and I divorced and my heart continued to ache but I sensed that all would be okay. I had to have faith. And without knowing it I was drawing closer and closer to the Divine Source. To make a long story short, once I figured out how the Law of Attraction works, let me tell you, my life has completely turned around. I remarried a wonderful man who had two children of his own. We had full custody of all four children, and the cost of daycare exceeded what I brought home in my paycheck, therefore, it did not make sense for me to work. I was able to stay home with our children! My oldest daughter was halfway through her kindergarten year, and I was now able to drop her off and pick her up. Something I had never had the chance to do before! And I was extremely grateful each and every day. It was easy for me to stay in the place of gratitude because it was sincere. We didn't know how we would survive financially without my income but survive we did and actually even better than we had before, although we had huge amounts of debt that we each carried over from our previous marriages. We joined a church and became involved in Bible studies to learn as much as we could. My heart and mind were transformed slowly. I started seeing things differently. I saw all things from love. We took a Financial Peace University course offered by Dave Ramsey which teaches a biblical way of dealing with money. We learned how to cut costs and be disciplined. Within two years we had paid off all of our credit card debt along with two personal loans. Our children thrived, and so did our relationship. I started my writing business, and that started to thrive as well. I can't begin to tell you how my life has turned around since I started practicing the Law of Attraction. We are blessed in so many surprising ways now, and so often, that we have come to be expectant of it. And we are grateful beyond measure.

ABOUT SAGE WILCOX

Sage lives in the United States with her husband of 15 years, children, cat, and dog. She is a certified energy healer and is working on becoming a Life Coach. Sage enjoys giving advice to her clients, friends, and family on healing, love, and relationships. She also enjoys studying human behavior, reading, writing, being outdoors, and enhancing her relationships with others. She enjoys growing closer to the Divine Source and reading and learning the Bible and scripture. In her experience, the more she learns and practices the Word, the better her life becomes.

Sage is a hopeless romantic! She strives to help others fall madly in love with everything about their lives! That includes all things most people would consider boring. There's no room for boring in Sage's life. She likes to spice life up in every way!

Other Books By Sage Wilcox:

Love Letters from Exes: Proof That Life Goes On After a Break Up and Love Is What You Make It

Until We Fall

The 2-Hour Vacation: Let Go and Relax, Reduce Stress & Anxiety, Gain Inner Peace, and Happiness

Please visit her website at:
http://sagewilcox.wix.com/books

If you have other ideas or want to share your success stories, please feel free to send me an email at: *sagewilcoxbooks@gmail.com*
I look forward to hearing from you! Thanks!

Disclaimer

The purpose of this book is for entertainment purposes only. This book is designed to provide information and motivation to our readers. The content of each article, letter, or insight is the sole expression and opinion of its author, and not necessarily that of the publisher. The letters contained in this book are from contributors and are the contributor's recollections of their experiences. This is a work based on opinions, recollections, and true events, however, names, characters, businesses, places, and incidents are either the products of the authors' imaginations or used in a fictitious manner. Any resemblance to actual persons, living or dead, businesses, companies, events, locales, or actual events is entirely coincidental. This book is not intended nor is it implied to be a substitute for professional medical advice, and any medical advice and any medical information contained in this book is not intended to be diagnostic or treatment in any way. The author and publisher are not engaged in rendering medical, psychological, legal, or any other professional services. If medical, psychological or other expert assistance is required, please talk to your physician and locate the services of a competent professional. The author and publisher shall have neither liability nor responsibility to any person or entity with respect to any loss or damage caused, or alleged to have been caused, directly or indirectly, by the information contained in this book. Neither the publisher nor the individual author(s) shall be liable for any physical, psychological, emotional, financial, or commercial damages, including, but not limited to, special, incidental, consequential or other damages. Our views and rights are the same: You are responsible for your own choices, actions, and results. If you do not wish to be bound by the above, you may return this book along with a copy of the receipt to the publisher for a full refund.

www.ingramcontent.com/pod-product-compliance
Lightning Source LLC
Chambersburg PA
CBHW070648050426
42451CB00008B/312